OXFORD
INDIA SHORT
INTRODUCTIONS

INDIAN FEDERALISM

The Oxford India Short
Introductions are concise,
stimulating, and accessible guides
to different aspects of India.
Combining authoritative analysis,
new ideas, and diverse perspectives,
they discuss subjects which are
topical yet enduring, as also
emerging areas of study and debate.

OTHER TITLES IN THE SERIES

For more information, visit our website:
https://india.oup.com/content/series/o/
oxford-india-short-introductions/

OXFORD
INDIA SHORT
INTRODUCTIONS

INDIAN
FEDERALISM

LOUISE TILLIN

OXFORD
UNIVERSITY PRESS

OXFORD
UNIVERSITY PRESS

Oxford University Press is a department of the University of Oxford.
It furthers the University's objective of excellence in research, scholarship,
and education by publishing worldwide. Oxford is a registered trademark of
Oxford University Press in the UK and in certain other countries.

Published in India by
Oxford University Press
2/11 Ground Floor, Ansari Road, Daryaganj, New Delhi 110 002, India

ISBN-13 (print edition): 978-0-19-949561-0
ISBN-10 (print edition): 0-19-949561-0

ISBN-13 (eBook): 978-0-19-909787-6
ISBN-10 (eBook): 0-19-909787-9

Typeset in Bembo Std 11/14.3
by Tranistics Data Technologies, New Delhi 110 044
Printed in India by Nutech Print Services India

To my father, Clive.
In loving memory.

Contents

Contents

Tables

Tables

Abbreviations

AFSPA	Armed Forces Special Powers Act
AGP	Asom Gana Parishad
BDO	block development office
BJP	Bharatiya Janata Party
BJS	Bharatiya Jana Sangh
CPI	Communist Party of India
DMK	Dravida Munnetra Kazhagam
FDI	foreign direct investment
FRBM	Fiscal Responsibility and Budget Management
GDP	gross domestic product
GST	goods and services tax
GTA	Gorkhaland Territorial Administration
IAS	Indian Administrative Service
ISC	Inter-State Council
J&K	Jammu and Kashmir

MGNREGA	Mahatma Gandhi National Rural Employment Guarantee Act
MGNREGS	Mahatma Gandhi National Rural Employment Guarantee Scheme
NDA	National Democratic Alliance
NDC	National Development Council
NITI Aayog	National Institution for Transforming India Aayog
OBC	Other Backward Class
PDS	public distribution system
PMJAY	Pradhan Mantri Jan Arogya Yojana
SVD	Samyukta Vidhayak Dal
TDP	Telugu Desam Party
UDAY	Ujjwal Discom Assurance Yojna
UPA	United Progressive Alliance
USA	United States of America
VAT	value added tax

Acknowledgements

Writing a short introduction like this without the standard architecture of academic references leaves many intellectual debts under-acknowledged. The bibliography at the end of the book tries to rectify that.

I have learnt much over the years from discussing Indian federalism and the politics of Centre–state relations with friends and colleagues including, among others, Yamini Aiyar, Balveer Arora, Katharine Adeney, K.K. Kailash, James Manor, Suhas Palshikar, Indira Rajaraman, Smitana Saikia, Rekha Saxena, and Wilfried Swenden. Serving as an editor of the journal *Regional and Federal Studies* since 2016 has also allowed me to engage closely with the latest comparative research on territorial politics and federalism.

Warm thanks to the team at Oxford University Press, India, for commissioning this short introduction and for steering it through the editorial process. Generous and incisive comments on the initial proposal and the final text by two anonymous reviewers have also been invaluable.

Lastly, thanks as always to Simon, and to our daughter, Beatrix, for putting up with my trips away and all the mysterious 'work' I do on the computer.

Introduction
India's Federal Model

Federalism rests on an idea of shared and multi-layered sovereignty enshrined within a particular configuration of political institutions. In federal systems, at least two levels of government—in India's case, the Centre and the states—share in the task of governing but have their own spheres of autonomy. Their joint and individual roles are typically protected by a written constitution, with a Supreme Court serving as an umpire in case of disputes.

Federalism has enabled the expression and protection of diverse forms of belonging within India and has been central to the richness and resilience of India's democracy. It is difficult to imagine a country of India's scale and societal diversity being governed without compromises over the sharing of decision-making rights and administrative responsibilities amongst tiers of government at the all-India and regional levels. Yet, some of the biggest dilemmas facing India today arise from the complexities and ambiguities generated within the resulting federal order.

In order to get to the bottom of how policies are made and the impacts they have in India's complex multi-level political and economic ecosystem, an appreciation of federalism is essential. The ability of the central government to promote economic dynamism or reduce inequality between regions, or the ability of India's states to define and resource their own policy agendas that speak to local needs and priorities, is shaped by federal institutions and practice. Questions such as how to achieve a balance between regional political, fiscal, and administrative autonomy, and the scope for authoritative policy making by the central government are some of the thorniest issues facing India today.

India's Unique Approach

India's model of federalism reflects the circumstances in which it was created in the aftermath of Partition and in an era when the need for strong central governments able to steer national development plans was influencing the design and reform of federal systems in other countries.

The heavily centralised order that India's constitutional architects opted for in the aftermath of the partition of the subcontinent departed radically from earlier visions of a decentralised federal model for India in which the central government's role would have been restricted to a small number of nationwide subjects and provinces empowered. India designed a federal system in order to share power with provinces. But strong measures were put in place to maintain the authority of the central government, and to allow for the operation of more unitary powers in times of emergency. Reflecting this, the word federalism does not appear by name in the constitutional text. As Dr B.R. Ambedkar said on introducing the draft constitution to the Constituent Assembly, the constitution was federal to the extent it introduced a 'dual polity' in which the Centre and the states each have sovereign powers exercised in fields established by the constitution. But the flexibility inherent in the Indian constitution distinguished the proposed Indian model of federalism from all that had gone before:

All federal systems including the American are placed in a tight mould of federalism. No matter what the circumstances, it cannot change its form and shape.

It can never be unitary. On the other hand …
[India's] Draft Constitution can be both unitary as
well as federal according to the requirements of time
and circumstances. In normal times, it is framed to
work as a federal system. But in times of war it is so
designed as to make it work as though it was a unitary
system…. Such a power of converting itself into a
unitary State no federation possesses. This is one point
of difference between the Federation proposed in the
Draft Constitution, and all other Federations we know
of. (Ambedkar 1948)

The Constituent Assembly had designed a model to
enable the central government to act fast with relatively
few checks in instances where internal or external crises
threatened stability. The constitution also enshrined a
model of strong interdependence between the central
government and states that was intended to push both
levels of government to work together to resolve issues
of national importance.

For these reasons, India's form of federalism has
sometimes been held up as a diminished version of
the 'real thing'. From the time the constitution was
crafted, observers described it as a 'quasi-federal'
system because of the weak protections it appeared
to offer to the autonomy of states compared to
other federal systems. India stands out from other
classic federal systems such as the United States of

America (USA) that were forged after formerly independent territories pooled their sovereignty and designed a model of federation that would protect their autonomy. There have been many instances over time in which India's central government has, in more and less egregious ways, compromised the autonomy of states. However, it is also clear that India has defined its own constitutional practice of federalism rather than following earlier blueprints.

India's form of federalism is best seen as an original rather than a derivative or diminished form. It is a centralised model with a strong degree of interdependence between the central government and the states. But it has a permissive approach to constitutional amendment providing flexibility to tackle issues, especially those concerning the accommodation of diversity that could prove much more intractable in a more rigidly interlocked federal system.

Over time, India has also become more genuinely 'federal' as a result of political and economic change. In the early decades, the dominance of the Congress party nationally and across states helped to bind the Indian Union together. The greatest tensions between the central government and the states emerged in the subsequent period during which Congress dominance was challenged. Centre–state relations, and calls for greater regional autonomy, formed part of the platform around which opposition to Indira Gandhi's leadership coalesced in the 1970s and 1980s. The ensuing parallel processes of economic liberalisation and political regionalisation from the late 1980s increased the centrality and autonomy of states in political and economic life. The involvement of regional parties alongside national parties in coalition governments at the Centre from the 1990s also enhanced the extent to which regional voices were represented in the central government.

India is today often seen as a model for emulation, or learning from, by newly federalising countries looking at ways to accommodate societal diversity. India's experience of federalism has also helped to counter some of the more pessimistic proclamations of those who have drawn from the failed experiments with federalism in the former Soviet Union or Yugoslavia to argue that internal borders should not be drawn along ethnic or linguistic lines, as India's have been since the first linguistic reorganisation of state boundaries in southern India in the mid-1950s. By extension, federalism—or the pursuit of 'unity in diversity'—has informed the image of itself that India has projected in international diplomacy in recent decades as a country whose own internal diversity (see Table I.1) serves as a bridge between countries.

Table I.1 Diversity of India's States

State	Population (million)	Largest Language	Literacy Rate (%)	GDP per capita (lakh rupees)
Sikkim	0.6	Nepali	81	2.7
Mizoram	1	Mizo	91	1.3
Arunachal Pradesh	1.4	Nyishi, Adi	65	1.2
Goa	1.5	Konkani	89	3.8
Nagaland	2	Multiple	80	0.9
Manipur	3	Meitei (Manipuri)	79	0.6
Meghalaya	3	Khasi, Garo	74	0.7
Tripura	4	Bengali	87	0.8
Himachal Pradesh	7	Hindi	83	1.5
Uttarakhand	10	Hindi	79	1.6
Jammu and Kashmir	13	Kashmiri	67	0.8
Delhi (National Capital Territory)	17	Hindi	86	3.0
Haryana	25	Hindi	76	1.8
Chhattisgarh	26	Hindi	70	0.8
Punjab	28	Punjabi	76	1.3
Assam	31	Assamese	72	0.7

(Cont'd)

Table I.1 (*Cont'd*)

State	Population (million)	Largest Language	Literacy Rate (%)	GDP per capita (lakh rupees)
Jharkhand	33	Hindi	66	0.6
Kerala	33	Malayalam	94	1.6
Telangana	35	Telugu	67	1.6
Odisha	42	Odia	73	0.7
Andhra Pradesh	50	Telugu	67	1.2
Gujarat	60	Gujarati	78	1.6
Karnataka	61	Kannada	75	1.6
Rajasthan	69	Hindi	66	0.9
Tamil Nadu	72	Tamil	80	1.5
Madhya Pradesh	73	Hindi	69	0.7
West Bengal	91	Bengali	76	0.8
Bihar	104	Hindi	62	0.3
Maharashtra	112	Marathi	82	1.7
Uttar Pradesh	200	Hindi	68	0.5

Source: Population, literacy, and languages (2011 census). NB. Literacy rate for Andhra Pradesh/Telangana is pre-bifurcation; per capita net state domestic product (at current prices) for 2016–17 (except Tripura 2015–16), RBI 2017–18.

Note: States are listed by population size (smallest to largest).

As former prime minister Manmohan Singh said in his Independence Day speech in 2007:

> The success of a secular democracy in a nation of a billion people with such diversity is viewed with admiration. This great idea of India as a symbol of unity in diversity is increasingly viewed with respect and regard. Our tolerance, our capacity to assimilate and our ability to reconcile the irreconcilable are objects of wonder.... Today, we enjoy good relations with all major powers and all developing countries. We have emerged as a bridge between the many extremes of the world. Our composite culture is living proof of the possibility of a confluence of civilizations. India will always be a nation bridging the many global divides. (Singh 2007)

Yet, the simultaneous political and economic decentralisation of the 1990s and 2000s also threw up the old challenges of how to ensure balanced regional development and to incentivise different parts of the country to contribute to the dynamism of the national economy. The emergence of multi-party governments in which the parties in power at the Centre and in the states were often incongruent, and during which national and regional parties shared in the task of government formation in

New Delhi, had increased the complexity of governing India from the Centre.

Paying attention to the constitutional, political, and economic dimensions that affect the relationship between the central government and the states in India, this short introduction seeks to stimulate an understanding of the development and functioning of India's federal model. The book's main focus is the Centre–state relationship. The analysis does not extend to a detailed examination of democratic decentralisation to the third tier of local government or panchayati raj institutions, although this has been another important part of the landscape of decentralisation from the 1990s.

The book begins by looking at the origins of federal ideas in India, including the development of provincial governments under British colonialism as well as the debates about Centre–state relations that occurred in the Constituent Assembly. Chapter 1 investigates why those debates, taking place in the aftermath of Partition, eventually led to the adoption of a comparatively centralised but nonetheless flexible vision of federalism that provides the constitutional framework for Centre–state relations to date. It also looks at the way that regional interests are represented at the Centre, especially in the Rajya Sabha (Council of States), the delineation of the respective powers of the Centre and the states, and the choice of parliamentary, rather than presidential, federalism.

Chapter 2 reflects upon the role of India's flexible federal model in providing institutional recognition to societal diversity, preventing linguistic conflicts, and contributing to the stability of Indian democracy. Over time, the evolution of federalism in India has allowed for a degree of self-governance for regional linguistic communities, preventing language from becoming a major source of conflict within the Indian body politic. India has also experimented with a range of approaches to conflict settlement that have grafted new forms of autonomy for minority ethnic communities onto the constitutional structure. The creative adaptation of federalism to accommodate the claims for recognition and decision-making of groups from Kannada, Tamil, or Telugu speakers in southern India to Mizos in north-eastern India has been essential for India's ability to hold together in its diversity.

However, the chapter also explores the limits of the extent to which the Indian approach to federalism has embraced divergent views of what membership in the Indian Union should entail. States that sit on India's border with Pakistan, not least Jammu and Kashmir (J&K), as well as parts of

11

the Northeast, have seen their membership of the Indian Union as often secured by coercion as by accommodation. Various 'asymmetric' devices that offer different degrees of autonomy to regions such as J&K, as well as some states in Northeast India, have in some instances been honoured more in the breach, and in others have raised new concerns about the rights of sub-state minorities in states where a particular community has been given a privileged form of recognition.

Chapter 3 turns to the question of how the pattern of Centre–state relations affects the practice of governing India. In many ways, the constitution placed a strong onus on cooperation between the central government and states to jointly tackle the pressing challenges of social and economic development that lay before India in 1950. The rhetoric of cooperative federalism has circulated in and out of political fashion since then, but all central governments have been faced with the question of how to work effectively with the states to pursue national goals. The central government has across time been a pre-eminent arena for policy formulation, but it has always depended crucially on the state-level administration for implementation. The state level has loomed even larger in the political and economic lives of India's citizens and businesses since the 1990s. Problems of state capacity that affect the routine implementation of national policies are endemic in many states, but elsewhere divergent policy preferences can also throw up Centre–state tensions and give rise to distinct subnational policy cultures. State governments face the challenge of representing local needs and preferences while working within a shared policy framework where central resources frequently come with strings attached.

Numerous institutional devices have been designed to facilitate or incentivise better cooperation between the Centre and states, but the most important feature determining the outcome of intergovernmental relations is arguably the party system. This chapter thus considers the ways in which changes in the wider political environment have shaped the operation of Centre–state relations over history.

Chapter 4 deals with the parallel question of how economic change has transformed the operation of federalism and vice versa. Economic liberalisation in India entailed the dismantling of centralised economic planning. State governments took centre stage in the ensuing race to entice private capital, both domestic and international. Economic decentralisation is often held to promote the dynamism of markets. Central governments since liberalisation have sought to encourage competition between states as a means of incentivising them to attract investment. But the extent to which inter-state competition is driving economic dynamism in India is open to question. Regional inequality has increased since the onset of liberalisation, and the gains of greater exposure to the global economy have been captured by a handful of states. Furthermore, local politics and political economic factors frequently drive state governments to take decisions that are at odds with the idea that competition between states for investment will drive macro-economic stability and produce 'business-friendly' environments. Rural sectors continue to be influential in state-level politics, producing countervailing pressures on reform agendas and raising distributive questions that state governments address in different ways.

Until very recently, there was a general consensus that India was moving gradually along an irreversible process of greater federalisation, a process that had been spurred by party system change, economic liberalisation, and social change, with urbanisation and growing penetration by regional media houses contributing to the consolidation of distinctive regional cultures within the constituent states of the Union. These features have all strengthened India's 'federalism in practice' over some of the more limiting features of the constitution. Yet, the recent shifts back towards a scenario of one-party dominance since the Bharatiya Janata Party's (BJP)'s national election victory in 2014 throw into sharp relief the underlying features of India's constitution and unsettle the notion that federalisation is a linear process in India.

India's federal constitution is a parliamentary model that empowers an executive selected from, and primarily responsible to, the lower house of the legislature. Territorial representation is relatively weak—when states have found a greater voice at the Centre, it has been as a result of their political empowerment more than their constitutional standing. When political power is consolidated in the hands of a single party, the checks that arise from the compulsions of coalition government do not function. Governments with parliamentary majorities in Delhi are able to govern in quite different ways to coalitions. If the 1990s and 2000s were decades where states were at the centre of the action—the primary focus of voters, with regional parties key players in holding together national coalitions—the 2010s have been a decade of renewed centralisation, especially since the ascendancy of the BJP under Prime Minister Narendra Modi since 2014. A brief Conclusion, therefore, reflects on some of the challenges facing federalism in India in the current era.

1

Constitutional Design

The Indian constitution was written between 1946 and 1949. It was the output of a generation of political leaders who had led the new nation to independence from colonial rule, but was also indelibly shaped by the traumatic aftermath of the partition of India and Pakistan. The task of nation-building rested heavily on the Constituent Assembly's shoulders. Above all, the architects of India's constitution sought to prevent any future rupturing of the new Indian nation. The constitution was designed with an eye on the goals that the leaders of the new nation saw before themselves, those of social and economic progress. These circumstances and ambitions profoundly shaped the character of the political institutions framed by the Constituent Assembly.

The resulting institutional design enshrined a pattern of power sharing between a central government and regional governments that was protected by a written constitution. But the new model of federalism crafted by the Constituent Assembly departed in marked ways from other federal constitutions that had been established before the mid-twentieth century in the USA, in Switzerland, and in other former British colonies such as Australia and Canada as they transitioned to dominion status within the empire. In fact, the constitution itself does not use the word federal or federalism, marking its clear departure from 'classic' models of federalism, even if the Indian model today is increasingly regarded as an important type of federalism in its own right.

In important ways, the constitution appeared to violate what had, until then, been seen as a cardinal feature of federal constitutions: the idea that the federal and regional governments should each have independence in their own sphere of authority. The model adopted in India, sometimes described as one of 'cooperative federalism', centred on the belief that the Union and state governments should be interdependent. Many of the critical nation building tasks were seen as requiring a role for the central government, even where the state governments would need to be key partners in their design and implementation. They were, therefore, included in the extensive concurrent list of the constitution, where powers are shared between

17

the central government and the states. Beyond this constitutionally enumerated shared domain, the Union government was also constitutionally empowered to act in, and even take over, the execution of policies in the domain of the states in situations of emergency, and on routine matters under certain conditions. The states were also made heavily dependent on the central government for revenue transfers; to this day, they lack independent revenue raising powers to finance their full set of responsibilities under the state list.

There is relatively weak representation of state interests at the Centre. States are represented on the basis of their population—not on an equal basis—in the second chamber of India's Parliament, the Rajya Sabha. While the Rajya Sabha reflects the partisan composition of state legislative assemblies which elect it, it mirrors the territorial composition of the lower house, which means that large states dominate by virtue of their size. The Rajya Sabha has become more powerful in periods of incongruence between political coalitions at the Centre and electoral patterns in the states, something that was more common after 1989. But on the whole, it does not act as a distinctive space for discussion of states' interests vis-à-vis each other or the Centre. This set-up makes India look very different to presidential federations such as the USA or Brazil where the equal representation of states in the

Senate introduces a different pattern of representation compared to their lower houses, giving small states equal representation to their larger counterparts.

Lastly, while it is clear that India has an indestructible Union, the borders of its states are themselves violable. Under Article 3, the Union government has the power to alter the boundaries of an existing state through division of its territory, or addition or removal of certain territories. These powers can be initiated by the approval of a simple majority in Parliament; they do not require approval by the state(s) concerned.

These features of the Indian constitution all impart a centralised character that at times veers closer to a unitary government. They qualify the idea of an independent sphere of authority for the states, and led observers at the time of the constitution's framing, such as the constitutional expert K.C. Wheare, to classify India as a 'quasi-federal' system. Yet, this term has always risked treating India's constitutional model as a diminished version of something else, rather than a model in its own right. Furthermore, it misses the fact that in many ways the kinds of hybridity that were intrinsic to the Indian constitution were also emerging in other longer-established federal systems in the same period. In other federal systems too, the problems of the mid-twentieth century gave rise to a greater role for central governments in initiating new approaches to social security and economic planning as they moved away from laissez faire capitalism to build new welfare states.

The unitary-like elements of the Indian constitution have also given it a flexible character, which have—perhaps unexpectedly—contributed to the further federalisation of the Indian polity over time. Measures such as the linguistic reorganisation of states, which have been critical for the recognition of minority rights and federal stability, would have been more difficult in a more rigid, interlocked model of federalism that protected an existing balance of power among states. Over time, they have contributed to the emergence of a more genuinely federal polity reflective of India's great societal diversity.

Factors That Shaped the Design of Federalism

While the constitution is decidedly a product of the particular circumstances and vision of the political elite of newly independent India, it was informed by close knowledge of other constitutions. The framers of India's constitution carefully studied other federal constitutions as they developed their own plans. They also retained many of the features of the

Government of India Act of 1935, which was the first constitutional model to be implemented in India that included something resembling an architecture of federalism, even if one that was heavily qualified by India's diminished sovereignty under colonialism. The Montagu–Chelmsford Reforms that led to the Government of India Act of 1919 followed by the Government of India Act of 1935 were introduced by the British in response to growing nationalist demands. The Acts introduced successive models of limited self-governance at the provincial level. The 1935 Act in particular sought to accommodate the rival nationalisms professed by the Muslim League and the Indian National Congress by proposing a federal model which placed residuary powers with the provinces in order to allow fulsome autonomy for Muslim majority areas of the country. It also proposed a model of federation between the British Provinces and the 560-odd princely states.

Only the first part of the Government of India Act of 1935, which gave autonomy in certain domains to provincial governments, was ever implemented. The first elections to new provincial legislative assemblies in British provinces were held in 1936–7 on a limited but expanded franchise that also included propertied women as voters for the first time. The advent of the Second World War put negotiations with the princely states about entry into a federation into abeyance. So it was only after Independence—under conditions of full suffrage and following the accession of most princely states to the Union, but with the loss of most Muslim-majority areas to Pakistan due to Partition—that a full-fledged Indian model of federalism came into being.

It is impossible to understand the factors shaping the approach to federalism taken by the Constituent Assembly without addressing the impact of Partition. At the outset of the Assembly's deliberations in December 1946, Nehru had introduced an Objectives Resolution, proposing the key contours of a future constitution at a time when it was still hoped that the Muslim League would join the Constituent Assembly. In order to appeal to the Muslim League, the Objectives Resolution envisaged a heavily decentralised federation with residuary powers remaining with the provinces. After the announcement of Partition in June 1947, the Union Constitution Committee of the Constituent Assembly rapidly moved to adopt a centralised federal model in which residuary powers would lie with the Union government. This centralised vision was designed with the intention of deterring any future threats to the integrity of the new Indian nation after Partition.

Another distinctive feature of the circumstances that gave rise to the Indian constitution, in contrast to other earlier federations, was that it was not the product of a bargain between previously independent polities opting to pool their sovereignty. The decision to federalise involved granting self-rule within a carefully specified domain to provinces that had previously been governed from the Centre under British colonial rule. While the eventual integration of the princely states did involve the fusing of entities with different prior status, this integration was not the result of equal bargains with the hundreds of individual states.

The result was that, as the constitutional scholar Granville Austin described, the constitutional negotiations resembled the members of a family in possession of their own house for the first time, working out how to live together (Austin 1966, 192). Political scientists refer to the federal system that emerged from these negotiations as an example of a 'holding together' federation as distinct from a 'coming together' federation such as the USA. In reality, the integration of the princely states also involved an element of 'putting together', given that force was used where necessary to integrate regions that resisted incorporation.

In Ambedkar's words, the constitution's Drafting Committee had opted for the word Union rather than federation because:

> The Federation was not the result of an agreement by the States to join in a Federation ... the Federation not

being the result of an agreement, no State has the right to secede from it. The Federation is a Union because it is indestructible. Though the country and the people may be divided into different States for convenience of administration the country is one integral whole, its people a single people living under a single *imperium* derived from a single source. (Ambedkar 1948)

Federalism is therefore not mentioned by name in the Indian constitution. But since 1994, it has been legally recognised as part of the constitution's basic structure which cannot be amended. Federalism was recognised as part of the 'basic structure' by the Supreme Court in *SR Bommai* v. *Union of India*, 1994, and *Kuldip Nayar* v. *Union of India*, 2006. But as the chief justice said in the *Kuldip Nayar* ruling, while 'the federal principle is dominant in our Constitution and that principle is one of its basic features ... it is also equally true that federalism under the Indian Constitution leans in favour of a strong Centre'.

Demarcation of Union and State Authority: 'Cooperative Federalism'?

By the mid-twentieth century, there was a growing recognition that federal systems premised on the principle of two levels of government operating independently of each other were ill–suited to respond to some of the new challenges of the post–war world. In the USA, the idea that the federal government should do more to protect people from the vagaries of market forces and unfettered capitalism gained ground following the Great Depression of 1929. The New Deal that followed, and mobilisation for the Second World War, further strengthened belief in the role of the federal government and the need for intergovernmental cooperation. Calls for 'cooperative federalism', with a larger role for the central government, grew with campaigns against racism, sexism, and urban poverty.

As governments in many parts of the world crafted new forms of social security and social insurance as part of new post–war compacts with their populations, it was recognised that heavily decentralised federal systems faced unique problems. Competition between provinces or states within decentralised federal systems undermined the initiation of policies such as unemployment insurance, health insurance, or old age pensions that disadvantaged local employers because they imposed costs on employers or had to be financed through increases in local taxation. Furthermore, provinces were unevenly endowed with abilities to raise tax and thus achieving inter-regional equity in a decentralised federation was difficult. Increasingly, federal countries such as Australia, Canada, and the USA began to see more active forms of central government intervention in distributive questions. Sometimes this involved new powers being granted to the central government such as responsibility for old age pensions in Canada, and in most places it involved the increasing dependence of regional governments on financial transfers from the central government, and the use of conditional grants by the federal government to promote progress in policy areas that were constitutionally the domain of the states.

In India, an appreciation of these emerging issues was hardwired into the constitution from the outset. Some form of federalism was seen as essential in India given its scale and diversity (although the units of the federation did not effectively represent that diversity until the linguistic reorganisation of states in the 1950s). But the form of federalism that was designed effectively enshrined many of the emerging practices of intergovernmental collaboration in other federations at the heart of the constitutional order, rather than strictly preserving independent spheres of authority for the Union and state governments. While the phrase 'cooperative federalism' was not used in the constitution, contemporary observers such as A.H. Birch and Austin described the resulting constitutional order in these terms. The language was also used by the Sarkaria Commission on Centre–state relations in its 1988 report, which stated:

By the middle of the Twentieth Century, federalism had come to be understood as a dynamic process of co-operation and shared action between two or more levels of government, with increasing inter-dependence and Centrist trends. The framers of the Constitution took due note of these changing concepts and functional realities. Avoiding a dogmatic approach, they fashioned a sui generis system of two-tier polity in which the predominant strength of the Union is blended with the essence of co-operative federalism. (Government of India 1988, Chapter 1, clause 1.3.28)[1]

The Indian constitution divides zones of responsibility between the central government and the states on the basis of three lists contained in the Seventh Schedule: the Union, state, and concurrent list (Table 1.1). The Union government is responsible for issues that affect India as a whole including war, internal security, macro-economic stability (including currency, foreign exchange, international trade, banking, insurance, and operation of stock exchanges), and the provision of public goods that are nationwide in scope (such as railways, communications, national highways, air transport, atomic energy, space, oilfields and major

[1] This is otherwise known as the Sarkaria Commission report.

Table 1.1 Distribution of Competencies

Union	State	Concurrent
Defence; armed forces (including deployment of armed force in aid of civil power in any state); atomic energy; foreign affairs; entering into/implementing international treaties or agreements with foreign countries; citizenship; railways, national highways, national waterways, maritime shipping, and airways; communications (broadcasting, post, telephones); currency; foreign loans; Reserve Bank	Public order; police; prisons; local government; public health and sanitation, hospitals and dispensaries; pilgrimages; agriculture; water (water supplies, irrigation and canals, drainage and embankments, and others); land (land rights, tenure, transfer, collection of rents, etc); industries (except where necessary for war or where Union control has been deemed in public interest); trade and commerce within state;	Criminal law and procedure; preventive detention; marriage and divorce; transfer of property other than agricultural land; contracts; bankruptcy and insolvency; prevention of cruelty to animals; economic and social planning; trade unions, industrial and labour disputes; social security and social insurance; welfare of labour; education (since 1976); legal, medical, and other professions; charities and charitable institutions; trade and commerce in industrial products deemed by parliament to be in

of India; interstate trade and commerce; banking; insurance; stock exchanges and futures markets; establishment of standards of weight and measure; Union Public Services; constitution, organisation, and powers of Supreme Court; income taxes (other than agricultural income); customs duties; corporation tax; jurisdiction and powers of all courts except Supreme Court with respect to matters in this list

money-lending; elections to the state legislature; state public services; land revenue; taxes on agricultural income; sales taxes (except newspapers); taxes on entry of goods into local area for consumption or sale; taxes on luxuries; jurisdiction and powers of all courts except Supreme Court with respect to matters in this list

public interest, foodstuffs, cattle fodder, raw cotton, and jute; price control; factories; electricity; newspapers, books, and printing presses; jurisdiction and powers of all courts except Supreme Court with respect to matters in this list

Source: Constitution of India, Seventh Schedule.
Note: This is an indicative, not an exhaustive list.

minerals, interstate trade and commerce, and regulation of interstate rivers). The states were given responsibility for issues such as local government, education, public health, and agriculture that were seen as best administered by a local tier of government, close to the point of implementation. They also have jurisdiction over public order, prisons, and policing.

The extensive concurrent list then covered issues in which both the Union and state governments took an interest. These were areas where it was deemed that national coordination was important in order to facilitate national planning, where national uniformity was desired or where it was anticipated the Union government may need to encourage the states to take action. The concurrent list contains Economic and Social Planning, Trade Unions, industrial and labour disputes, social security and social insurance, labour welfare, as well as criminal law, marriage, divorce, and other family issues among other subjects. The constitution left scope for some provincial entrepreneurship in the concurrent domain: state legislation can prevail over central legislation but only if it has been passed later and received approval from the president.

In fiscal terms, the constitution also enumerates the allocation of taxation powers between the Centre and the states. The most significant taxes were allocated to the Centre, including taxes on income and wealth from non-agricultural sources, corporation tax, taxes on production, and customs duty. The states were allocated a host of other taxes. The most important today are sales tax, state excise, and stamp and registration fees. However, these taxes were not expected to be sufficient to meet states' expenditure responsibilities. Therefore, the constitution also provided for a system of Centre–state transfers overseen by an independent Finance Commission appointed every five years. The Finance Commission proposes formulae for the distribution of centrally levied taxes, as well as grants from the Consolidated Fund of India to the states. Thus, in fiscal terms, the states are locked into a model of financial interdependence with the Union government in order to perform even those activities that are constitutionally assigned to them.

Over time, other mechanisms have also been created to channel resources from the central government to the states, and in an attempt to bring states into line with national goals. Between 1950 and 2014, the Planning Commission allocated grants and loans to the states to support their development plans, which nested within the five year planning cycles of the Planning Commission at the all-India level. In addition, central ministries have been able to make grants directly to the states either as 'central sector projects' fully funded by the Centre, or as 'centrally sponsored schemes' match-funded by the states. These centrally sponsored schemes increased in scope from the 1970s and often dealt with subjects that were constitutionally allocated to the states.

Thus, the constitution envisaged, and sought to facilitate, intergovernmental collaboration. In its more unitary like provisions, it also empowered the Union government to routinely enter the domain of the states to facilitate national coordination and preserve national unity.

For instance, the constitution offers ample scope to Parliament at the Centre to legislate on matters in the state list, where they relate to the implementation of international treaties or agreements (Article 253), when a national emergency is in operation (Article 250), on other matters deemed to be in the national interest, if a resolution permitting this is passed by two-thirds of those present and voting in the Rajya Sabha (Article 249), or if two or more state legislatures request Parliament to legislate on a common matter (Article 252).

Parliament also supersedes state legislatures where a subject can be read in the Union list, even if it appears in the state or concurrent list. For instance, under centralised industrial planning, the central government directly regulated many industries, even though industries are constitutionally a state subject. It could do so via entry 52 of the Union list which allows Parliament to legislate with regard to industries where Parliament declares their control by the Union to be 'expedient in the public interest.' By the 1980s, the list of industries deemed to be in the public interest included the production of razor blades, gum, matchsticks, pressure cookers, bicycles, and zip fasteners. This situation led constitutional lawyer A. Nani Palkhivala to exclaim in 1984 that 'without amendment of the Constitution, "Industries" has been nefariously transformed into a Union subject and has ceased to be a State subject' (Prasad 1985, 18). The dominance of the Union Parliament over state legislatures has generally been upheld by the Supreme Court in cases that dispute the interpretation of overlap between the lists, or the application of residuary powers (Singh 2016).

Beyond the effective dominance of the Union government over state governments in terms of legislative powers, the central government under Article 356 also has the right to declare President's Rule in a state where it is deemed that the government cannot govern 'in accordance with the provisions of the Constitution'. These emergency powers—much abused for political reasons up until the mid-1990s— have been some of the most controversial features of the constitution.

Lastly, as we have seen, Article 3 permits the central government to redraw the boundaries of any constituent state of the union without the approval of its state legislature. Such a measure would be unthinkable in a 'states rights' federation such as the USA, where the sanctity of the boundaries of the federating units are a core tenet, and where the composition of the Senate makes it much harder for any changes to the composition of the federation to occur because it would alter the existing balance of power among states.

Ambedkar argued that granting broad powers to the Union government and adopting a permissive approach to constitutional amendments (except for those that altered the balance of powers or revenues between the Centre and states) offered flexibility in contrast to the problem of rigidity seen in other federal systems. The flexible nature of the constitution has in many ways facilitated its longevity and enabled responsiveness to changing circumstances.

Territorial Representation and Parliamentary Federation

Having explored the respective spheres of authority of the Union government and the states, and the ways in which central power can be and has been deployed under the constitution, it is worth asking what influence the states have in the formulation of Union policies via representation at the Centre. Constitutionally the main way in which states are represented at the Centre is in the upper chamber of Parliament. The nature of state representation, and their powers at the Centre, is also shaped by the fact that India is a parliamentary federation in which the executive (the prime minister and his/her cabinet) is directly responsible to the lower house.

Parliamentary and presidential systems interact with federalism in different ways. Presidential systems such as the USA and Switzerland are based upon a separation of powers between the executive and legislature. In both the USA and Switzerland, there are two equally powerful houses in the federal legislature based respectively on representation by population, and the equal representation of the territorial units. By contrast, in parliamentary federations the relationship between the executive and legislative is fused, with the executive directly responsible to the legislature. In these systems, the role of the second chamber is typically more limited. This is partly because cabinet is responsible to the lower house, and because the second chamber (not directly elected) is intended to be a revising chamber rather than a competing centre of gravity. Some authors suggest that it is the parliamentary tradition built on strong cabinet rule that gives rise to majoritarian tendencies in India, as opposed to countries in which federalism serves as a means for checking the power of the executive branch of government.

India's states are represented in the Rajya Sabha on the basis of their population. They are indirectly elected by members of state legislative assemblies. This model follows that proposed in the Government of India Act of 1935, as well as the Nehru Committee Report of 1928. Relatively little consideration was given during constitutional debates of the 1920s and 1930s to the idea of a federal second chamber with equal representation of states. The Nehru Report simply concluded that because members of the upper house would be elected by provincial legislatures, provinces would feel that they were represented at the Centre. It is not clear why equal representation for the states did not receive greater attention during the subsequent Constituent Assembly debates. One reason may be that the provinces were not coming together as formerly independent polities pooling their sovereignty in the constitutional negotiations. Furthermore, the provinces were of vastly different sizes. Another factor, as Austin (1966) suggested, may be the fear that equal representation for all constituent units would ultimately have led to the provinces being sidelined by the princely states which were far greater in number.

The Rajya Sabha does, however, have important powers as a second chamber, and most Constituent Assembly members saw its role predominantly as a revising chamber that would be able to reflect coolly on measures passed by the popularly elected lower house. The Rajya Sabha can also initiate legislation (except for money bills which it can neither originate nor reject) and it must discuss the budget. Its members sit on parliamentary standing committees, and it has an effective veto on constitutional amendments. But when there is deadlock between the two houses, a joint session of both houses of Parliament can be called. This has only occurred three times in India's history (1961, 1978, and 2002), but has allowed the Lok Sabha to overrule opposition from the Rajya Sabha. The Sarkaria Commission agreed that the Rajya Sabha's main role was as a second legislative chamber, exercising coordinate functions with the Lok Sabha rather than representing the 'federal principle'.

The Rajya Sabha is granted the powers to speak for the states on certain issues: for instance, allowing Parliament to legislate on matters in the state list in the national interest, or calling on the Union to create an all-India service. But the Rajya Sabha is a fairly weak forum for representing states' interests vis-à-vis the Centre. Because states are represented on the basis of their population rather than on an equal basis, the territorial pattern of representation within the Rajya Sabha essentially mirrors the Lok Sabha. Rajya Sabha MPs are typically more likely to vote on party lines rather than form coalitions based on state interests, even when—as the Sarkaria Commission showed—they are voting on measures under Article 249 that extends the Union's ability to vote on matters in the state list.

It is worth noting that the distribution of parliamentary seats in both houses of Parliament has been frozen since a constitutional amendment in 1976 during the Emergency. This measure was introduced in an attempt to incentivise states to reduce population growth by adopting family planning initiatives, and not to penalise those states that were more successful in doing so. The effect of this freeze over time has been to marginally over-represent southern states such as Tamil Nadu, Karnataka, and Kerala that have reduced population growth, and to under-represent larger northern states such as Uttar Pradesh, Rajasthan, and Madhya Pradesh. The under-representation of the latter states also means that the representation of Scheduled Castes or Dalits via allocation of reserved parliamentary seats is lower than it otherwise would have been because Dalits are more numerous in the northern states. India's very small states in the Northeast and the centrally governed union territories are also over-represented because they are each allocated one MP, regardless of population size. This situation violates the principle of one person, one vote, because it generates parliamentary constituencies of vastly different sizes (ranging from 48,000 in the union territory of Lakshadweep to 3 million people in Malkajgiri, Andhra Pradesh). However, the degree of what political scientists call 'malapportionment' is considerably less than other federal systems such as many in Latin America or the USA where states are represented on an equal basis in the upper house regardless of population size.

The territorial element of representation in the Rajya Sabha has become further attenuated in recent times, a move legitimised by the Supreme Court. In *Kuldip Nayar* v. *Union of India*, 2006, the petitioner—a former Rajya Sabha member—argued that a 2003 amendment to the Representation of the People Act, 1951, violated the principle of federalism in the constitution because it removed the requirement that a candidate for elections to the Rajya Sabha must be an 'elector for a Parliamentary constituency in that State or territory'. The amendment to the act had stated that candidates in Rajya Sabha elections could be electors anywhere in India: they did not need to reside in the state which they would represent in the upper house. In the ruling, the Supreme Court upheld federalism as part of the basic structure of the constitution, but strikingly argued that 'in the context of India, the principle of federalism is not territory related'. The chief justice drew a contrast between India and other federal constitutions with bicameral central legislatures such as the USA and Canada whose constitutions— unlike India's—set out residence requirements for the Senate. The chief justice cited Ambedkar's emphasis on the essential aspect of federalism in the constituent assembly: 'The chief mark of federalism as I said lies in the partition of the legislative and executive authority between the Centre and the Units by the Constitution' (Singh 2016).

Thus, at least in terms of constitutional design, the role of the Rajya Sabha in representing territorial interests is limited. There are ongoing calls for its reform, including by the M.M. Puncchi Commission Report on Centre–state relations in 2010 which recommended the repeal of the amendment to the Representation of the People Act nullifying the residency requirement for Rajya Sabha MPs, as well as a move to a system of equal representation of the states to protect the rights of smaller states. Such a change is hard to imagine, however, since it would involve larger states voluntarily voting away their power in favour of much smaller and politically less powerful states.

The Rajya Sabha does, however, play a role in representing the status quo, and status quo ante, in the state legislatures. The extent to which this bolsters the Rajya Sabha's power depends on wider dynamics in the party system. Given that state legislatures have been elected according to a different timetable than the Lok Sabha in most states since the 1970s, and given the increased divergence between electoral outcomes across the two levels, this has imparted a different character to the composition of the upper house compared to the Lok Sabha—at least since the days of Congress party dominance—and has, in some periods, reinforced its role as a counterweight to the lower house.

In terms of its constitutional design, then, Indian federalism is Centre-heavy and based on a model of interdependence between the Centre and the states in fiscal and administrative terms. The fact that India adopted a parliamentary model of federalism also led to a smaller role for the second chamber in representing territorial interests. In some ways, the centralised model of federalism has increased its flexibility because it does not provide institutionalised protection to a particular balance of power among states as federating units. However, the constitution itself also offers fairly weak protections against central incursions into the domain of the states. This has meant that the nature of Centre–state relations is heavily determined by changes to the balance of electoral power within the party system.

2

Federalism and Diversity

The last chapter documented some of the extensive powers enjoyed by India's Union government, and qualifications on the extent of self-rule enjoyed by its state governments. The centralising tendencies of the constitution also have implications for the management and accommodation of societal diversity. Yet, the very diversity of India also makes it extremely hard to envisage India as a unitary polity. As Congress politician, N.V. Gadgil said to the Constituent Assembly: 'It is impossible to govern a country so big, with so many traditions and with such a variety of cultures with about two hundred and twenty different languages and to bring them in one administrative unit in the sense that there would be one unitary State, one legislature and one executive' (Constituent Assembly of India Debates, 18 November 1949).

This idea of India as one country encompassing a wealth of cultures, languages, and traditions has become a central pillar of India's national identity. The notion of 'unity in diversity' is a trope by which India understands itself and projects its identity on the world stage. The survival and relative stability of the Indian polity, in spite of its diversity, is itself remarkable. These things distinguish India's experience from the fate of other continental size projects such as the Soviet Union and Federal Republic of Yugoslavia, or from other post-colonial federations such as that in Nigeria that have seen severe instability and in some cases state break-up.

There are a number of ways in which India's federal system has changed over time which have helped to accommodate diverse ways of belonging within the country. Ironically perhaps, the strong prerogatives of the central government and weak institutionalisation of states' rights in the upper house have endowed the Indian federal system with a strong element of flexibility that has proved essential in managing conflict and preventing the emergence of stronger fissures. This has especially been the case with the reorganisation of state boundaries along linguistic lines, as well as the design of some asymmetrical constitutional features in India's Northeast, which offer protections to the autonomy of minority ethnic groups. However, the use of territorial devices to recognise the rights of minority religious communities, including Muslims, Sikhs, and Christians, has a much more vexed history. National security concerns have often trumped accommodative impulses in India's border regions.

Accommodation of Diversity

At the point of Independence, it was India's first prime minister, Jawaharlal Nehru, who exerted the strongest influence on the territorial design of the new Indian state. For Nehru, who was concerned with crafting a machinery of government to lead the new nation towards economic and social progress, a strong centralised apparatus was crucial. This strong Centre was to be the vehicle for state-led industrialisation, and also for the social integration and rehabilitation of the vast flows of refugees from Pakistan. A new modern India was to be built through heavy industries, steel plants and dams, and the new cities that were to emerge within a centralised model of national economic planning. In this context and after the trauma of Partition, Nehru sought to avoid giving succour to any social forces that risked impeding the foremost task of consolidating the new nation. In one of his early fortnightly letters to chief ministers in January 1948, Nehru wrote that the rehabilitation of refugees from Pakistan is 'a colossal problem and requires the fullest cooperation of the whole of India in solving it. This necessitates cooperation and coordination under central direction' (Nehru 1948, 35).

Apart from Partition, the other pressing task in terms of the territorial organisation of the state was the integration of the 560-odd former princely states with the provinces of British India. The princely states ranged from tiny specks on the map to large territories with their own governance arrangements. The task of integration was overseen by the first deputy prime minister of India Sardar Vallabhbhai Patel, and involved amalgamating the princely states with the former British Provinces or forming small clusters. This process resulted in the creation of three categories of states: Part A, B, and C states with differing degrees of autonomy from the central government. The borders of the political map of India in 1950, when the constitution was promulgated, were those that had arisen from this process of integration. These borders had a good degree of continuity with the territorial structures developed under British rule.

Only a few of the former British provinces were organised according to a linguistic principle. The British had conceded demands from regional language lobbies for a new province of Orissa in 1936, meaning that in eastern India Oriya speakers and Bengali speakers had their own states. But in much of India, the British provinces were multilingual entities. Telugu and Tamil speakers coexisted in Madras, Gujarati and Marathi speakers in Bombay, and Hindi and Marathi speakers in the Central Provinces and Berar. Many of the larger princely states were also multilingual. The vast state of Hyderabad in southern India encompassed speakers of Kannada, Marathi, Telugu, and Urdu.

Congress had reorganised its own party structure during the 1920s to accommodate the sentiments of regional linguistic communities such as Oriya, Tamil, Telugu, and Marathi speakers. However, at the point of Independence, Nehru set the idea of creating linguistically homogenous states to one side. He feared that the elevation of language would give way to parochial, inward-looking forms of provincialism that at their most extreme could imperil national unity. Two reports by a Linguistic Provinces Commission set up by the Constituent Assembly and a Congress committee (named the 'JVP' committee after its members, Jawaharlal Nehru, Sardar Vallabhbhai Patel, and Pattabhi Sitaramayya) recommended that no new provinces should be created at a time when national unity was the paramount concern.

Yet, within a few years, pressures for linguistic states grew. Rising peasant castes such as the Kammas and

Reddys, and the Lingayats and Vokkaligas pushed demands for linguistic states. The Communist Party of India (CPI) threw its weight behind the demand for a Telugu-speaking state. In December 1952, Potti Sriramulu died while on hunger strike demanding a Telugu-speaking state. As riots broke out, Nehru was pushed to concede the creation of Andhra Pradesh as well as setting up an independent commission to review other statehood demands. In 1956, the States Reorganisation Act created new states according to language in Karnataka, Kerala, and Madhya Pradesh. These were followed in 1960 by the creation of Maharashtra and Gujarat from the erstwhile province of Bombay, and in 1966 by the division of Haryana and Punjab. The redrawing of state borders along the lines of linguistic community imparted a stronger multi-ethnic basis to its federal model.

State reorganisations have not been confined to linguistic demands. Since the 1970s, India's Northeast— in particular its largest state of Assam—has been substantially reorganised to recognise autonomy claims of members of various tribal communities such as Nagas and Mizos. This phase of reorganisation involved asymmetric devices that have given a measure of security to some larger ethnic minorities within the Northeast, but created cascading demands for commensurate recognition by other groups in the region.

The predominantly Hindi-speaking region of north and central India has also been reorganised. This reorganisation created new states where there had been long-running demands for statehood grounded on critiques of the socio-economic and political marginalisation produced within prevailing state-level political economies. In this vein, a long-running demand for a tribal state of Jharkhand, carved out from Bihar to combat a situation of 'internal colonialism', was finally conceded by the BJP-led central government in 2000. Yet, statehood was granted at a point in time when the tribal population of Jharkhand had become a minority. The statehood demand had been pursued vigorously by the BJP in the 1990s as the party sought to establish a foothold in the region by appealing both to Scheduled Tribes (the traditional constituency for statehood) and the many non-tribal communities who had migrated over generations to the region to take advantage of economic opportunities. The extent to which the eventual grant of statehood accommodated tribal demands, in these circumstances, or facilitated a better stake in decision-making for tribal communities has therefore been questioned.

Also in 2000, under the BJP-led coalition government at the Centre, the state of Uttarakhand—encompassing the hill region of Uttar Pradesh—was created. The creation of a hill state had been a long-running demand in the hills to combat perceived marginalisation at the hands of planners in the plains. However, the demand gained momentum following the advent of new reservation policies for lower castes or Other Backward Classes (OBCs) across Uttar Pradesh which would have adversely affected the hill areas. The hill areas have a peculiarly low proportion of OBCs and a much higher than average population of upper castes. In this context, the BJP also stepped up its support for the creation of Uttarakhand, which was eventually created including substantial plains districts alongside the hills. The BJP also supported the creation of a third new state, Chhattisgarh, where there had been relatively little popular mobilisation and which was carved out from Madhya Pradesh. All three of these states were created at a period in time when politics across the Hindi heartland states was being transformed by the rising political clout of lower castes. A politics of lower caste assertion altered the political geography of electoral power in these states and provided opportunities for new political entrepreneurs and parties to find ground by provoking and/or supporting new statehood demands.

In 2014, in a further indication of the fluidity which political regionalisation has imparted to the territorial structures of the Indian federal system, the state of Andhra Pradesh was divided to realise another long-standing demand for a state of Telangana. As with the states created in 2000, the demand for Telangana had an ethnic dimension but one that was also couched within a critique of patterns of domination within the regional economy. Residents of the Telangana region, which had been merged with other Telugu-speaking regions to create Andhra Pradesh in 1956, had long argued that residents from coastal Andhra had been able to dominate economic opportunities in the state by virtue of their historical advantages derived from investment in irrigation in rural areas and their higher levels of education and literacy. Despite measures intended to protect the position of Telanganaites within government employment in Andhra Pradesh, complaints about the socio-economic domination of coastal Andhra persisted. However, the translation of these historic grievances into the actualisation of a demand for statehood owed much to the changing fortunes of the major political parties in the state. Fearing the complete loss of its support base in the state following the untimely death of its popular chief minister Y.S. Rajasekhar Reddy, and the inept handling of appointing a successor, the Congress party at the Centre eventually committed itself to creating the new state of Telangana. It did so after a hunger strike by the leader of the main regional separatist party threatened to unleash a new wave of popular mobilisation.

The relatively frequent reorganisation of state boundaries in India reflects the flexibility of the Indian constitution. New states can be created on the basis of a simple parliamentary majority, without constitutional amendment. There is no requirement to secure the agreement of the elected legislative assembly of a state to be divided. In fact, the case of Telangana in 2014 shows that a central government—when minded to—faces no constitutional barriers to the creation of a new state even in an instance where there is strident opposition from the parent state. In this regard, India's federal model looks quite distinctive. In most other federal systems, the region concerned would have to consent to bifurcation. Furthermore, because state creation in India does not affect the balance of power between other states—as it would in countries where federal sub-units have an equal voice in a territorial upper chamber—proposals to create new states have not faced blocking coalitions led by other states in Parliament. These features have been important in enabling federalism in India to evolve in order to accommodate diversity. Article 3—often cited as a qualification to the notion that India has a federal polity—has in fact enabled the central government to use reorganisation as a means of accommodating diversity in a way that has contributed to the strengthening of the federal elements of India's constitution.

Most crucially in terms of the overall stability of the Indian federal system, the linguistic reorganisation of state boundaries has helped to prevent language emerging as a singular line of political identification or conflict. Had linguistic states not been conceded, language could have become the basis for solidifying support for secessionist demands. Rather than proving an impetus for the unravelling of the federal system, as pessimists such as Selig Harrison had predicted in the late 1950s, linguistic reorganisation helped to provide security to dominant linguistic communities within India's regions. Through recognition of different linguistic identities, and by allowing linguistic communities to determine their own official language policies within their state once they had states of their own, the creation of linguistic states helped to alleviate potential tensions between an Indian national identity and regional identities shaped profoundly by language.

The creation of linguistic states also helped to activate other lines of identity within electoral politics. Once speakers of Tamil, Telugu, or Kannada had their own states, they began—as political scientist James Manor observed—to focus on 'all that divided them: caste, class, sub-region, urban versus rural residence, and so on. The solidarity essential to secessionism could never flourish under such circumstances. Ever since, heterogeneity within each linguistic region has been the bulwark of national unity' (Manor 1998, 25).

Yet, even with linguistic reorganisation, language had the potential to be a source of tension in Centre–state relations for as long as the possibility remained that Hindi could be imposed as the sole national language. While state legislatures were able, under Article 345 of the constitution, to adopt any one or more languages in use in the state for official purposes, the compromise enshrined in the constitution established Hindi with the Nagari script as the official language of the Indian Union, but with a temporary period of 15 years in which English would also remain an official language. Opposition to Hindi becoming the sole national language in the 1960s on expiration of this sunset clause was particularly fierce in Tamil Nadu. Tamil opposition led to an important amendment of the Official Languages Act in 1967. The amendment ensured that states that had not adopted Hindi as their official language would be able to continue to use English in their communications with the central government and with other Hindi-speaking states, and that government and parliamentary papers would be published in both Hindi and English.

Linguistic reorganisation, in addition to the 1967 compromise over the national language, helped India to become a more genuinely multinational federation in which major linguistic communities had acquired important rights of self-governance, as well as a veto on a mono-national interpretation of India's official language. Yet, as the latter examples of reorganisation since 2000 have shown, the impulses governing reorganisation have not always been straightforward acts of accommodating diversity. The comprehensive exercise of examining the bases for statehood in the Indian Union has not been repeated since the States Reorganisation Commission in the 1950s. Since that time, decisions about when and where to create new states have been shaped by opportunities generated by the changing party system, more so than a clear set of principles about the structure of the state.

Furthermore, as scholars such as John McGarry and Brendan O'Leary argue, the more centralised, unitary-like aspects of India's constitution can appear like forms of devolution by the central government rather than an equal bargain between national or ethnic communities. They argue that a model of devolution leaves ultimate power with the central government which can be in the hands of the dominant nationality or ethnic community, rather than securing a 'plurinational partnership of equals' (McGarry and O'Leary 2011). For this reason, they—and others—have argued that India does not have stronger protections for minorities characteristic of 'full pluralist federations'. These protections would include a constitutionally protected division of powers which cannot be unilaterally rescinded, substantive autonomy for sub-units including in the allocation of fiscal resources, consensual—rather than majoritarian—decision-making rules within federal government including proportional representation and proportional allocation of public posts and resources, and a strong second chamber that is not simply a mirror image of the lower house. The intergovernmental distribution of powers in India does not approximate this stronger definition of 'plurinational' federalism.

The extent to which power-sharing has occurred in practice has depended on India's party system as much as its formal constitutional set-up. Arend Lijphart (1996) made an exception to his famous theory of consociationalism to suggest that India had embraced core tenets of power sharing despite the absence of formal power-sharing mechanisms in the constitution, such as grand coalition, proportionality, or minority veto. Lijphart argued that under Nehru, the Congress party at the Centre served as a conduit for minority representation in ways that achieved the goals of power-sharing without formal institutional mechanisms. However, others have disagreed with this portrayal. Steven Wilkinson (2000) argued that far from being inspired by a commitment to power-sharing with ethnic minorities, the Congress party under Nehru sought to be 'colour blind'. It was only after Nehru's death and the institutional decay of the Congress party in the 1960s that a range of new parties emerged representing middle and lower castes. Since then, India has become more proportional in terms of both political representation and public sector employment, driven by the desire of political entrepreneurs to attract newly mobilised minority and lower caste voters. However, the increasingly consociational nature of political life in this period has enhanced, rather than diminished, ethnic violence.

It has also been difficult for minorities that do not share a common language or numerical preponderance within a given region to achieve recognition via the reorganisation of state boundaries or to protect their autonomy at a sub-state level. The creation of a state such as Jharkhand, for instance, occurred only once the tribal population had become a minority, and the statehood demand had become a vehicle for a much wider set of interest and identity groups. The ongoing demand to carve out a state of Gorkhaland for Nepali-speaking communities in the northern-most hill districts of West Bengal reflects not only the allure, but also uncertain promise of achieving statehood in the face of strident sub-nationalism of a dominant regional community. Tripartite talks between sub-state movements, state governments and the central government have produced sub-state autonomous councils in a number of states including West Bengal. But the Darjeeling Gorkha Hill Council and subsequent Gorkhaland Territorial Administration (GTA) have been starved of resources and autonomy. Since 2014, Bengali sub-nationalism has been resurgent as West Bengal chief minister, Mamata Banerjee, has sought to strengthen her position in opposition to the Centre under Narendra Modi, and to resist the incursions of the BJP into West Bengal. The announcement in May 2017 that Bengali would be made a compulsory language in schools across the state triggered a fresh wave of unrest in the Nepali-speaking districts. Short of achieving demands for statehood, sub-state minorities face relatively weak protections in the face of majoritarian tendencies at the state level.

Asymmetry: The Possibility and the Limits of Accommodation

The discussion above highlights the importance of the reorganisation of state boundaries as a means of facilitating the coexistence of multiple identities within the Indian state or what Stepan, Linz, and Yadav (2011) call the Indian 'state-nation' to recognise the extent to which this embrace of multiple identities has become constitutive of the Indian state. But our discussion has not yet touched on the question of how far India's federal system has evolved in order to embrace divergent views of what membership in the Indian Union should entail. India, like many other multi-ethnic polities, has experimented with asymmetric devices that offer different levels of autonomy or self-governing rights to particular regions with a distinctive identity or history of Centre–region conflict.

The Indian constitution today contains several forms of asymmetry. First, several provisions grant stronger degrees of autonomy to certain regions (Fifth and Sixth Schedules; Article 370 with regards J&K, Article 371A for Nagaland, and Article 371G for Mizoram). Second, Articles 370 and 371 include provisions for positive discrimination intended to mitigate inter- or intra-state inequality.

Jammu and Kashmir is the only state of the Indian Union which negotiated a special status at the point of accession, and which continues to have its own constitution today. The Hindu maharaja of this Muslim-majority region, Hari Singh, acceded to India on very limited grounds in October 1947 in return for military support against a tribal uprising against his rule. This act of accession drew the Indian and Pakistani armies into their first military confrontation, ending with a ceasefire in January 1949 which established the present-day Line of Control between Indian and Pakistani administered

Kashmir. In the first instance, Kashmir acceded to India only with regard to foreign affairs, defence, and communications. This state of affairs was confirmed by Article 370, which was negotiated for over five months by Nehru and the Kashmiri leader Sheikh Abdullah and included in the Indian constitution, albeit as a 'transitional' measure until a constituent assembly met in the state. Article 370 stipulated that the Indian Parliament could only exercise legislative powers in areas other than foreign affairs, defence, and communications on recommendation of the president and with 'concurrence' of the state government. The president could also cease or amend the operation of Article 370, but only on the recommendation of a constituent assembly in J&K.

Since 1954, an increasing number of constitutional provisions have been extended to the state, as a gulf has opened up between the gradual desire of prime ministers from Nehru onwards to integrate the state more deeply into the Indian Union and the desire of many Kashmiris to preserve a special status for their region. The extension of some constitutional provisions was approved by the state's constituent assembly in 1954—by then Sheikh Abdullah had been imprisoned—and many more have been extended since then. Today, Article 370 offers relatively weak safeguards of autonomy. A

State Autonomy Committee report published in 2000 called for Article 370 to be replaced by a new compact between the central government and the state, arguing that Article 370 has 'acquired a dangerously ambiguous aspect. Designed to protect the State's autonomy, it has been used systematically to destroy it' (Chowdhury 2000, 2599–603). Meanwhile, it has been a long-running demand of Hindu nationalists, including the BJP at a national level, to abrogate Article 370 and Kashmir's special status altogether.

In addition to Article 370, negotiations to end sub-state secessionist movements in parts of India's Northeast have resulted in autonomy arrangements for Nagas and Mizos under Article 371. These articles provide that unless the State Legislative Assemblies so decide, no act of parliament with respect to the religious and social practices of Nagas and Mizos respectively can be extended to the states. In both states, the Legislative Assembly can also restrict the application of any law related to the ownership and transfer of land. In Nagaland that provision extends to 'land and its resources', which has opened up a new frontier of Centre–state tension over who possesses the rights to regulate oil exploration in the state.

These regions with asymmetrical status in the constitution are all geographically remote from the majority Hindu, Hindi–speaking region of central and north India. While the Kashmir Valley is a majority Muslim region, Nagaland and Mizoram have substantial Christian populations. They are also borderland regions. Jammu and Kashmir sits on the border with Pakistan; Nagaland and Mizoram on the border with Myanmar. It is in these regions, as well as in Punjab, that India has seen its longest lasting secessionist movements. While the forms of constitutional asymmetry that have been negotiated for these regions in an attempt to moderate secessionist claims have sometimes been celebrated for institutionalising a commitment to diversity, there is a darker side to these forms of accommodation. The central response to regional demands in these states has also involved coercion and the maintenance of spaces governed by exceptional laws such as the Armed Forces Special Powers Act (AFSPA).

Indeed, some scholars have gone so far as to argue that far from reflecting a spirit of accommodation, the central government's approach to these regions has been one of 'hegemonic control'. Gurharpal Singh has argued that the Indian state has used the language of state and nation-building to expand into the peripheral regions through coercion and militarisation alongside mechanisms such as internal partition (redrawing boundaries of borderland states), co-option, creation of tribal zones and special territories, as well as attempted integration and assimilation (Singh 2001). Kashmir,

Punjab, and the Northeast have all seen frequent imposition of President's Rule, rigged or khaki elections, and counter-insurgency—all elements of the 'coercive instrumentality of democratic structures' in regions where secessionist demands arise (Singh 2001). Since the passage of an Anti-Secession Bill (giving rise to the sixteenth constitutional amendment) in 1963, every candidate for public office has also had to pledge to uphold the 'sovereignty and integrity of India'.

Likewise, Sanjib Baruah has described the AFSPA as a legacy of 'colonial constitutionalism'. This Act creates a localised and indefinite form of emergency rule, under which if an area is declared as 'disturbed', the armed forces can make preventive arrests, search premises without warrant, and shoot and kill civilians, while fundamental rights are essentially held in abeyance. The AFSPA first became a law in 1958 as armed forces began counter-insurgency operations against Naga rebels in Assam. The AFSPA has subsequently been extended to cover the whole of the Northeast (allowing the government to notify areas as 'disturbed') and to J&K. Baruah argues that this legal framework reflects the legacy of a colonial frontier mentality in these regions where emergency-like powers are routine and the military assists civilian power. National security concerns, from the first India–China war (1962) onwards, provided grounds for securing this frontier space, especially along the contested border with China.

The accommodative potential of federalism in the Northeast and J&K is thus curtailed by the fact that these are border regions in which national security concerns, as well as the potential for cross-border infiltration in support of secessionist groups, have often trumped core democratic tenets. But there is an additional reason why these regions have a more troubled position within the history of Indian federalism and this reflects the dominant position of minority religious groups within them.

The historical failure to agree a formula for protecting the rights of religious minorities within a putative Indian federation left the way open for the partition of the subcontinent in 1947. In the aftermath of the traumatic legacy of partition, the question as to how religious difference could or should be accommodated within the federal system has remained a vexed one. This has been especially difficult where a religious minority shares a religion with a neighbouring state with which India has hostile relations, most especially in the case of Kashmir and Pakistan.

After Kashmir's accession to India in October 1947, Article 370 was not agreed in order to recognise the state's distinct Muslim majority status or to embed group rights for Muslims via an asymmetric status.

It did not enshrine a constitutional commitment to a differentiated notion of citizenship within the Indian Union. Rather, Article 370 was a transitional compromise intended to postpone a final constitutional settlement pending resolution of the conflict in Kashmir and reference to a UN-mandated plebiscite. Nehru saw the Kashmir issue through the lens of secular nationalism and sought to resist attempts to paint the conflict in a communal light. Writing to chief ministers in January 1948, he stated: 'You will always remember that this Kashmir affair is not essentially a communal affair and that we are fighting side by side there with the Kashmir national movement under the leadership of Sheikh Abdullah' (Nehru 1948, 34). Abdullah himself argued that Kashmir's accession to India could help in defeating Hindu communalism and the threat that India might itself be converted into a religious state in the future (Bhattacharjea 1994, 189).[1]

For Hindu nationalists, Article 370 became a target for opposition from the outset. The Bharatiya Jana Sangh's (BJS)'s first manifesto in 1951 called for Kashmir's full integration into the Indian Union and opposed giving it a special position. Its 1957 manifesto called for 'nationalising all non-Hindus by

[1] Speech by Sheikh Abdullah at the inauguration of the J&K Constituent Assembly, 5 November 1950.

inculcating in them the ideal of Bharatiya culture' and for the amendment of the constitution to 'declare Bharat to be a Unitary state' (BJP, 2005). The BJS argued that many regional movements were being driven by foreign powers who, by supporting religious minorities, sought to destabilise India. In addition to the situation in Kashmir, the activities of Christian missionaries aroused their ire. While the BJS eventually made its peace with the linguistic reorganisation of states, it continued to vociferously oppose any form of federal reorganisation that appeared to appease minority religious groups. The accommodation of states such as Nagaland and Mizoram with a special constitutional status has long proved controversial for Hindu nationalists because it concedes too much to the idea of India as a multinational state.

The desire not to concede regional demands made by minority religious groups also extended to the Punjab, where Sikhs demanded a state of their own after Independence. As Paul Brass wrote in a major study of language, religion, and politics in North India, a set of written and unwritten rules have governed the form in which regional demands can be made, and which are defined as legitimate and subjects for accommodation, and those which are deemed illegitimate. One of these rules has been that 'regional demands based on language and culture will be accommodated, but that regional demands which are explicitly based on religious differences will not be accepted' (Brass 1974). Thus, demands for linguistic states were accommodated in the 1950s, but it was only after the demand for a Punjabi *suba* (state) was redefined along lines of linguistic rather than religious difference, that it was eventually conceded in 1966.

Indian federalism has evolved to provide institutionalised autonomy to linguistic minorities and given them a limited veto on the imposition of Hindi as an official national language of India. These innovations alone have helped strengthen the resilience of democracy in India. India has also experimented with granting forms of differential autonomy to certain regions as part of the negotiated settlements to regional conflicts, although these have had varying degrees of success. These asymmetric constitutional provisions have also been accompanied by routine coercive practices by the state in these border regions.

Thus, while linguistic accommodation has enhanced the multi-ethnic character of Indian federalism, the territorial management of diversity in India has not accorded similar recognition to all facets of identity and belonging. This chapter has highlighted the troubled history of accommodating religious minorities through territorial mechanisms.

Federalism has also offered relatively few safeguards to sub-state minorities, or those minorities that do not have numerical preponderance in particular territories. I have already briefly discussed some of the challenges faced by linguistic minorities such as Nepali speakers within West Bengal. Less often acknowledged are the implications of federalism for thinking about caste and gender relations.

The politicisation of caste—especially in north and central India—has also changed political imaginaries of territory. Shifts in the political sociology of representation from the 1970s provided the backdrop to the rethinking of state boundaries that resulted eventually in the division of Bihar, Madhya Pradesh, and Uttar Pradesh in 2000. Radical Dalit movements have, at times, also imagined creating Dalit majority enclaves through resettlement in order to challenge their perpetual minority status in territorial terms.

In other ways, the kinds of group rights privileged in autonomy arrangements have also created new dilemmas for gender politics. Autonomy arrangements have sometimes been used to defend patriarchal ideologies. The policing of women's conduct has on occasion formed part of a strategy of maintaining community cohesion. For instance, some tribal organisations in the state of Nagaland have vehemently opposed the attempted reservation of a third of posts for women candidates in municipal elections in line with the all-India legislation. In 2012, the Nagaland State Assembly passed a resolution rejecting women's reservations on the grounds that they threaten the social and customary practices of the Nagas which are protected by Article 371A. A 2016 Supreme Court bench upheld the ruling of the Gauhati High Court in favour of a petition by women's groups contesting the ban; but rather than settling the issue, this led to a fresh wave of unrest in Nagaland.

Groups that feel left behind by existing forms of distributive politics make special claims of their own, sometimes using violence to pursue their goals. This can take the form of a constant proliferation of new ethnic groups pressing claims on the state. In places where attempted settlements to conflict have introduced new forms of near zero-sum competition, such as in Bodoland in Assam, autonomy measures themselves—intended to recognise the claims of certain minority groups—can provoke new counterclaims by groups that find themselves newly marginalised. The Northeast in particular has seen cascading claims for group rights, which have been particularly thorny to resolve in areas of heterogeneous settlement.

To conclude, the constitution has offered a flexible framework for accommodating group demands, which was crucial for the reorganisation of state borders along linguistic lines. This element of flexibility enabled federalism to evolve in ways that have better represented and recognised some of India's cultural diversity. However, the territorial model of accommodating diversity has also had limitations, and has been more successful in some parts of India than others.

3

Governing India
Centre–State Relations

Federalism has sometimes been blamed for making India more difficult to govern. This may seem ironic given how far the constitution empowers the central government and has allowed it to encroach into the domain of the states. It is also a puzzling view since it neglects the importance of federalism in accommodating diversity and preventing the emergence of secessionist claims that could have loomed much larger as a source of instability. Yet, the fact remains that India's federal character expresses some of the fundamental compromises and challenges inherent in governing a complex, continental scale polity.

The central government faces the challenge of how to achieve policy coordination at an all-India level and resolve collective action problems across states with diverse identities, interests, and patterns of politics. State governments face the opposite challenge of how to exert influence at the Centre in order to influence the shape of national policies or to retain the autonomy (both political and fiscal) to set their own policy agendas.

Despite these sources of competition, the central government and states are constitutionally locked into a strong system of interdependence. Even in periods of political centralisation, the central government remains deeply reliant on state governments for carrying out its policies on the ground and for routine administrative matters. This gives considerable power to the states and creates challenges for the Centre in coordinating effective policy implementation throughout India. Meanwhile, the states remain fiscally dependent on the Centre. The pushes and pulls of Centre–state relations—which are above all driven by politics—are, therefore, central to understanding how the work of government is done, how policies are made, and how they are implemented.

Cooperative Federalism: Centre and States Working Together?

The Indian constitution was deliberately designed to move away from a federal model premised on distinct and exclusive spheres of autonomy for the central government and states. In legislative terms, the constitution designed a model of interdependence. First, it enumerated an extensive concurrent list in which both the central and state governments are able to legislate. Second, both levels of government were given power to legislate over specific sub-fields within the same policy area such as trade and commerce, which means that cooperation is required.

In fiscal terms, the states do not have sufficient revenue raising powers to carry out even those policies that are in their exclusive domain on the 'State list' of the Seventh Schedule. They therefore depend on fiscal transfers from the central government. These transfers come both as a formula-derived proportion of central taxation (via the Finance Commission), and as grants-in-aid or programme-specific transfers such as centrally sponsored schemes (either via line ministries or historically via the Planning Commission). These fiscal tools have been a major device used by the central government to influence and shape state-level activity. Many states have increased their own revenue take since the take off in economic growth in the 2000s affording them some cushioning of their own. However, on the whole, states remain heavily reliant on central transfers, especially the smaller hilly states and poorer states with weaker growth in their own revenues (Table 3.1).

Table 3.1 Sources of State Revenue (as Percentage of Total Revenue), 2016–17

State	Own Tax Revenue %	Share of Central Taxes %	Grants from Centre %
Nagaland	5	32	59
Mizoram	6	38	51
Arunachal Pradesh	6	71	18
Manipur	6	41	51
Meghalaya	13	44	35
Sikkim	14	45	31
Tripura	15	41	42
Jammu and Kashmir	19	23	49
Bihar	22	56	19
Assam	25	41	26
Himachal Pradesh	27	17	50
Jharkhand	28	41	20
Odisha	31	38	20
Uttar Pradesh	33	43	13
Chhattisgarh	35	35	19
Madhya Pradesh	36	37	19
West Bengal	39	38	21
Rajasthan	41	31	18

(*Cont'd*)

Table 3.1 (*Cont'd*)

State	Own Tax Revenue %	Share of Central Taxes %	Grants from Centre %
Uttarakhand	44	26	25
Goa	45	24	3
ALL STATES	*45*	*30*	*17*
Andhra Pradesh	45	27	24
Kerala	56	20	11
Punjab	58	20	10
Telangana	58	18	12
Gujarat	59	17	12
Tamil Nadu	61	17	14
Karnataka	62	22	12
Haryana	65	13	11
Maharashtra	67	16	11

Source: RBI 2018–19. Data for 2016–17 (Accounts).

Note: Table does not include non-tax revenue.

In terms of administration, the constitution gives wide scope to the states, although there are important structures for coordination. The all-India Indian Administrative Service (IAS) is a nationwide bureaucracy, recruited centrally with officers posted to state cadres. It is intended to facilitate communication between the Union and states and to ensure uniformity in administration, while being in touch with local conditions within states. When the colonial-era

Indian Civil Service was transformed into the IAS after Independence, its supporters also saw it as a force for maintaining national unity. Speaking in the Constituent Assembly, Sardar Patel argued: 'The Union will go–you will not have a united India, if you have not a good all-India service which has the independence to speak out its mind.... This Constitution is meant to be worked by a ring of Service which will keep the country intact' (cited in Government of India 1988, clause 8.7.06).

Indian Administrative Service officers form the apex of a much larger administrative structure that is recruited locally. While they were once seen as the eyes and ears of the central government at the state level, they have become deeply embedded within state bureaucracies, and at more senior levels work closely with chief ministers. They are just as likely today to be considered the eyes and ears of a state government when they are posted in Delhi.

In some areas such as railways, defence, foreign affairs, currency, customs and excise, and broadcasting, the central government has its own administrative machinery (the 'central services') to implement its laws at the state level. But for most matters on the concurrent list, and some other matters in the Union list, the central government relies on working with the state-level administrative machinery to carry out policies and implement government programmes.

Thus, even in the face of complaints that the central government has encroached on the legislative domain of the states, there is a strong degree of functional interdependence between levels of government when it comes to policy implementation. This situation leaves the central government dependent on state-level governments to faithfully implement national policies. This can be a major source of tension between the central government and the states, particularly when they are governed by different parties and/or when states are required to provide matched funding for central programmes. Such tensions often spill over into conflicts about who (the Centre or the states) receives the credit—or blame—for policy implementation.

State governments have sometimes come into deliberate conflict with the central government over the implementation of centrally designed policies, or they may more quietly drag their feet over implementation or fail to provide resources or autonomy to their local bureaucracies to facilitate effective implementation. Sometimes these dynamics are driven by vertical political competition between a party in power at the Centre and in a state. Other times, they may be explained either by weak state administrative capacity or by the fact that state governments have developed their own policy priorities and take their own decisions about where to invest their administrative energies in line with local political compulsions.

States lack institutional mechanisms to influence the design of a key type of central programme: centrally sponsored schemes. There are many complaints that such schemes are too inflexible or designed with a 'one size fits all' mindset, ignoring variation in local needs and preferences. The reality therefore is that it is in the implementation phase that states do most to shape and determine the effectiveness of central programmes. While the central government wants its schemes implemented by the states and noticed by voters, state governments face an often competing set of political incentives.

The central government is also faced with a situation in which administrative capacity varies hugely across states. If we set the politics of Centre–state relations aside for a moment and think of the central government as an altruistic or honest broker seeking to reduce regional inequality and alleviate poverty in the poorest regions, the central government operates in a scenario in which some state governments, especially those in many of the poorer states, lack the capacity to implement central programmes and spend central transfers intended to mitigate poverty. Indeed, there is evidence to show that poorer states spend less of their allocations from central government than richer states, despite having greater need (Mathew and Moore 2011). There are also huge numbers of personnel vacancies across India at the block level—the most local tier of the bureaucracy—which undermines administrative capacity to carry out routine developmental tasks.

Since policy making continues to be highly centralised and implementation highly decentralised, there is then a considerable mismatch between the ambitions of government and its ability to carry them out. As recent research by Aditya Dasgupta and Devesh Kapur (2017) suggests, local bureaucracies are under-staffed and over-burdened by a proliferation of government schemes and requirements as to planning, monitoring, and redressing local grievances. In an all-India survey conducted in 2017, they found that as many as 48 per cent of all approved full time positions in block development offices (BDOs), the frontline agencies for rural development schemes, lay vacant. As a result of this chronic under-staffing, block development officers who are responsible for the voluminous paperwork, form-filling, and reporting that is necessary to release funds for local activities from higher levels of government, in fact spend much of their time firefighting on the frontline. Their jobs are made more difficult by uncertainty about when higher levels of government will release funds for government schemes due to inefficiencies and manipulation of the architecture of managing financial flows from the Centre to the grassroots. It is these frontline agencies that are responsible for actually delivering on the flagship schemes of central government such as the Mahatma Gandhi National Rural Employment Guarantee Scheme (MGNREGS) introduced by the Congress–led United Progressive Alliance (UPA) government in 2005, or the Swachh Bharat programme against open defecation launched by the BJP-led National Democratic Alliance (NDA) government in 2014.

The constitution sets out a number of institutional mechanisms that are supposed to enable coordination between the Union government and the states. Under Article 263, the president can establish an Inter–State Council to investigate disputes between states, or to examine issues in which some or all states, and the Union, have an interest. An Inter–State Council was established in 1990, but it has been weakly institutionalised as a platform for managing intergovernmental relations. Parliament also has the right to adjudicate disputes relating to inter-state rivers or river valleys.

The introduction of the uniform goods and services tax (GST) across India in 2017 involved a new institutional innovation in the field of intergovernmental cooperation in the form of the GST Council. The central government and state governments jointly administer the GST via representation on the GST Council. The weighting of votes on the Council ensures that states will have to work with the central government (and vice versa) in order to reach agreement. This will introduce a new setting for intergovernmental cooperation, but it is too soon to judge its effects.

Thus, while India has a 'cooperative' model of federalism requiring intergovernmental collaboration in all sorts of fields, it does not have a well-developed institutional architecture for intergovernmental coordination or dialogue. Political party dynamics have been much more important in shaping the Centre–state relationship in this regard. This was as true of the era of Congress party dominance when intergovernmental disputes often became intra-party matters, as it has been of the subsequent period in which different parties governed at the Centre and in the states.

In order to understand the dynamics shaping intergovernmental relations, it is thus necessary to look at the changing nature of the party system. Centre–state dynamics have looked very different in periods when India has been governed by a single dominant party at the national level (Congress 1947–67; BJP 2014–) compared to periods in which there has been greater incongruence between the party/ies in power at the central government and in the states. Periods of incongruence include the premiership of Indira Gandhi (1967–84) during which the Congress largely remained dominant at the national level but faced a range of competitors at the regional level, of Rajiv Gandhi (1984–9), and the period from 1989–2014 during which no single party won a majority at the national level, prompting a range of experiments with coalition governments that brought some regional parties directly into the central executive for the first time. In the first period of incongruence, regional assertions provoked a centralising response from Prime Minister Indira Gandhi and increasing vertical Centre–state conflict. In the period between 1989 and 2014, the reality of governing in coalition brought a more accommodative approach, but it is not clear that regional parties were the strongest advocates for states' interests as a whole. In periods of greater congruence, intra-party mechanisms for Centre–state negotiation have been important. The remainder of this chapter will look at how changes within the party system have affected the operation of Centre–state relations over time.

Historicising the Politics of Centre–State Relations: Empowering the Centre in an Era of Planning

In the early 1950s, many observers, including Nehru, worried that the central government was not sufficiently empowered to take forward the task of social and economic development or the construction of a welfare state. In the early years after Independence, Nehru highlighted the apparent constraints on the scope of national authority. He was frustrated by the conservatism of the IAS, many of whose officers had simply been transferred over from the colonial era Indian Civil Services after 1947. But he was also worried about the Centre's authority vis-à-vis the states. Writing to chief ministers in August 1950, soon after the proclamation of the constitution, Nehru lamented that the central government 'is in the unenviable position of responsibility for everything without power to do much' (Nehru 1948, 156).

The American expert on public administration, Paul Appleby, wrote in 1953: 'No other large and important national government ... is so dependent as India on theoretically subordinate but actually rather distinct units responsible to a different political control, for so much of the administration of what are recognised as national programmes of great importance to the nation.' New Delhi's authority, he suggested, lay in 'influence rather than power' exercised through 'making plans, issuing pronouncements, holding conferences' rather than an administrative structure that enabled central ministries to oversee the recruitment and management of the organisations tasked with policy implementation (Appleby 1953, 18, 22).

Aside from emergency powers, the constitution appeared to place limits on the extent to which the central government could lead programmes of what Francine Frankel (2006) described as 'democratic social transformation'. The central government was better endowed with coercive powers than with permissive powers that would enable it to directly implement policies to improve well-being in line with the Directive Principles of the constitution.

Nehru's reflections about the limits on central power in his letters to chief ministers in 1950 were prompted by his perception that the response to food shortages in a number of states, especially Madras, Bihar, and Bombay, had been wanting. He expounded:

The Centre … gets all the blame and each State demands all kinds of help from the Centre all the time. But the Centre is not an inexhaustible storehouse for everything needed. It is only a co-ordinating factor drawing sustenance from the States. If the States fail to do their duty, the Centre cannot discharge its functions. There has been far too much slackness in some of the States, more especially those that are called surplus States (Nehru 1948, 157).

He complained that surplus states had not made any real attempt to procure surplus produce from farmers to redistribute to other states because of a fear of the electoral consequences of doing so: 'The result is that the State takes little trouble itself and throws the blame upon the Centre' (Nehru 1948, 157).

Nehru's analysis of the situation threw up classic issues faced by all federal systems: collective action problems, how to achieve inter-state redistribution, and vertical conflict or competition over the attribution of responsibility. In other important policy areas such as land reform, he also found his priorities subverted at the state level by chief ministers within his own party beholden to rural landed interests who resisted the application of ceilings on land ownership. His frustrations about the apparent constraints on the central government's ability to coordinate action at a national level lay behind the establishment of the Planning Commission in a cabinet resolution of 1950. The Planning Commission wrote and agreed on national and state five-year plans and gave advice on the disbursement of discretionary or non-statutory grants by the central government to the states. It was intended to bolster the central government's ability to plan for development at a national level.

By the mid-1950s, the Planning Commission's authority—and with it, that of the central government—had increased. As the Sarkaria Commission documented in the 1980s, the Union government in effect extended its powers including into areas that constitutionally were the exclusive domain of the states: 'Centralised planning through the Planning Commission is a conspicuous example of how, through an executive process, the role of the Union has extended into areas, such as agriculture, fisheries, soil and water conservation, minor irrigation, area development, rural reconstruction and housing etc. which lie within the exclusive State field' (Government of India 1988 clause 1.4.09). The Planning Commission's authority was certainly questioned. Much of the agrarian programme contained in the first Five Year Plan (1951–6) was heavily contested and in the end not implemented; but from the Second Five Year Plan (1956–61) onwards—when the focus on industrialisation was much stronger—the effect was one of centralisation in Centre–state relations.

Over-Reach and Counter-Reaction

While Nehru was prime minister, Congress remained the dominant party at both the Centre and the states. This meant that many Centre–state conflicts were effectively dealt with by intra-party channels. Coordination between the central government and chief ministers in the states were effectively intra-party negotiations. But this had started to change by the time his daughter, Indira Gandhi, became prime minister in 1966.

In the 1967 elections, the Congress party was defeated in a swathe of states. This ushered in a period of greater partisan incongruence between the central and state governments. Congress lost to a variety of parties: the Dravida Munnetra Kazhagam (DMK) in Madras, a left alliance in Kerala, a United Front-Left Front alliance in West Bengal, the Swatantra Party in Orissa, and coalition Samyukta Vidhayak Dal (SVD) or United Legislators Party governments in Bihar, Madhya Pradesh, Haryana, and Uttar Pradesh bringing together a combination of Jana Sangh, Swatantra, local parties, and Congress defectors.

The new non-Congress-ruled states made their voices heard after the 1967 elections, calling for a more formulaic approach to the disbursement of central grants than the discretionary approach hitherto followed by the Planning Commission. Their demands increased the proportion of formula-based transfers via the Planning Commission (using the Gadgil–Mukherjee formula). They also led to an expanded role for the National Development Council (NDC) (a forum of the prime minister, chief ministers, and members of the Planning Commission) in developing national plans. However, in practice, the NDC struggled to establish autonomy from the Planning Commission.

Two years later, Indira Gandhi initiated a split within the Congress party to assert her own authority over old party bosses. Adopting a populist style of leadership new to India, Indira Gandhi increasingly sought to appeal directly to the peasantry over the heads of local elites as she promised to eradicate poverty. She increasingly centralised power, bypassing existing institutions. This was the beginning of a much more conflictual era in Centre–state relations both within the Congress party and between Indira Gandhi's Congress party and opposition parties.

By the early 1970s, a range of new regional and social movements had emerged. In some places, these movements bolstered claims for greater regional autonomy. In 1972, the Jharkhand Mukti Morcha was formed taking on the mantle of a statehood demand for Jharkhand alongside a new form of 'red–green' activism. In 1973, the Akali Dal in Punjab published the Anandpur Sahib resolution calling for greater regional autonomy. These regional demands added to the range of mobilisation against government, culminating in the confrontation preceding the declaration of a national Emergency in June 1975.

Throughout this period, complaints were made by opposition-ruled states about central transgressions into their affairs. In 1971, the Rajamannar Committee Report appointed by the Tamil Nadu government to examine Centre–state relations recommended vesting residuary power with the states, repealing laws enacted under some provisions in the Union list, transferring a number of matters from Union and concurrent lists to the state list, removing Articles 356 and 357, and making amendments to secure the financial autonomy of states. The Anandpur Sahib resolution went even further to demand that central power be limited only to defence, foreign affairs, communication, railways, and currency. In December 1977, the West Bengal cabinet passed a resolution on Centre–state relations that expressed concern at the Centre's persistent efforts to erode the role of the states. It recommended that residual powers should be passed to the states, a reduction of some Union powers, and that the word 'federal' be inserted in the preamble to the constitution.[1]

---

[1] For details of these state-level reports and recommendations on Centre–state relations, see Prasad 1985, 19.

Indira Gandhi's tenure in office is remembered for many things, but in terms of Centre–state relations, two things stand out. First, the increased use—and frequently abuse—of coercive powers by the central government, and rising overt tensions between the central government and state governments that could not be settled within the framework of a dominant party system. Second, this was a new phase of 'development'-oriented interventions by the central government in the terrain of states.

In the 20 years until 1967, President's Rule (Article 356) had been declared a total of 10 times. There was a steep increase in the dismissal of state governments using Article 356 after 1967, including in many instances when a state government enjoyed a legislative majority or when no opportunity had been given to other parties to form a government. Indeed, the Sarkaria Commission calculated that of the 75 instances of President's Rule until 1987, only one-third had occurred when there was actually no alternative to direct rule by the Centre. Under Indira Gandhi, between 1967 and 1975, President's Rule was routinely used to deal with intra-party splits within local units of the Congress party, as well as applied in states ruled by opposition parties. It is worth noting that the Janata government elected after the Emergency was equally prone to the use of Article 356 against the remaining Congress governments in the states.

This was, then, a period of tension in Centre–state relations that can be understood as a response to the breakdown of a one-party dominant system and the emergence of Centre–state partisan incongruence as a norm.

On her post-Emergency return to power in 1980, Prime Minister Indira Gandhi took an increasingly interventionist and hard-line position against regional movements in Punjab and in Kashmir. Her ill-fated adventures in Punjab led to the storming of the Golden Temple in Amritsar to flush out militants she had previously sponsored to weaken the Akali Dal, the main opposition to the Congress. She was eventually to be assassinated by her Sikh bodyguards in 1984.

On the development side, from the late 1960s onwards, the central government via the Planning Commission oversaw an increasing array of 'centrally sponsored schemes' designed to tackle poverty reduction as Indira Gandhi made *garibi hatao* (poverty eradication) a central pursuit of her prime ministership. These are schemes that are implemented by state governments under the concurrent and state lists of the constitution, typically co-funded by the central government and the states. These again increased the more discretionary role for the central government in making fiscal transfers to the states, despite the move to a formula based model for Planning Commission transfers in 1967. They also represented movement by the central government into the constitutional terrain of the states. As Congress party dominance was challenged within the party system, the central government relied more heavily on the Planning Commission to exert control over the states.

While this was, in so many respects, an era of greater centralisation in Centre–state relations, it is striking that this era of heightened tension between the central government and the states also witnessed the beginning of greater policy innovation at the state level. Some of the new challengers to the Congress party at the state level, such as the Dravidian parties in Tamil Nadu and the Telugu Desam Party elected in 1983 in Andhra Pradesh, developed new state-level schemes as part of their appeal to state electorates. The Mid-Day Meal scheme—since 1995 a national scheme—began as an initiative of the Tamil Nadu chief minister, M.G. Ramachandran, in 1982. The new era of political regionalism was starting to throw up policy experiments among the states, some of which served as incubators for what would later become all-India policies.

Political and Economic Regionalisation

That one of Mrs Gandhi's late initiatives in office was to establish a new commission on Centre–state relations led by Justice R.S. Sarkaria was an indication of the clamour against centralisation and the need to adjust to the growing regional demands. Rajiv Gandhi's tenure in office between 1984 and 1989 marked the beginning of a more accommodative phase in Centre–state relations. As prime minister, he made tentative steps to sound a more conciliatory tone in some long-running regional conflicts. But there were also steps backwards, not least in Kashmir where rigged elections in 1989 sparked a new deep phase of conflict with the central government that remains unresolved.

It was the national elections of 1989 that marked the clearest turning point in Centre–state relations. For the first time since Independence, no national party was able to win a majority in the Lok Sabha elections. The issue of Centre–state relations and demands for greater regional autonomy had become a dividing line in politics at the national level, and helped to increase opposition unity against the Congress party. This was the beginning of a phase in which an accommodation of regional interests and actors had to take place at the Centre. It was also the eve of an even bigger transition in India's political economy. The dismantling of the central government's role in industrial licensing as a result of economic liberalisation and the opening up of the Indian economy to foreign investment was to give the states much greater autonomy over economic policy. Together, political regionalisation and economic liberalisation fundamentally altered the role of the Centre in India's political economy.

The political and economic empowerment of the states in the context of economic liberalisation, as well as the rise of regional parties and the growing primacy of the states in India's political life, inverted an earlier understanding of cooperative federalism under Congress party dominance. It became much harder to imagine that a cohesive national majority was the driving hand of policy decisions in Delhi. Instead, the parallel processes of political regionalisation and economic liberalisation, amid the dismantling of the centralised license permit raj, unleashed a more competitive form of federalism. Regional inequality increased as some states marched ahead and others— not favoured by their geographical location, political histories, social hierarchies, or long term stocks of human capital formation—fell behind. Observers spoke of a form of 'provincial Darwinism' in which the role of the central government as a guiding hand in India's federal market economy weakened and states competed with each other.

In 1989, a National Front coalition led by the Janata Dal under V.P. Singh bringing together a number of regional parties including the Telugu Desam Party (TDP), DMK, and Asom Gana Parishad (AGP), and supported by the BJP, defeated the Congress. It campaigned on a manifesto which demanded 'true federalism' meaning decentralisation and 'genuine autonomy' for the states. The Janata Dal was officially a national party in 1989 with a strong base in seven major states. The success of the National Front owed partly to the unpopularity of the Congress party that was engulfed in the Bofors corruption scandal, as well as better opposition coordination. It was not the moment that regional parties themselves increased their presence in the Lok Sabha (in fact the effective number of parties in the Lok Sabha fell between 1984 and 1989). But it is telling that the Janata Dal did not last long as a national party, soon breaking apart into a number of state-level parties which have since been important players in states including Bihar, Karnataka, Odisha, and Uttar Pradesh.

This heralded the beginning of a genuinely post-Congress polity in which the effects of a more fragmented and regionalised electoral landscape were felt at the Centre. As well as the splintering of the Janata Dal, the Congress party also splintered with breakaway parties forming in Maharashtra (Nationalist Congress Party), West Bengal (Trinamool Congress), and elsewhere which played a role in the crystallisation of new regional political arenas. New regional parties came to power for the first time in a number of North

Indian states representing lower castes, shattering the erstwhile dominance of the Congress party. The effects of this party system regionalisation were seen in a period of instability in government formation at the Centre. This included experimentation with a United Front minority government (1996–8), containing neither of the main national parties (Congress or BJP), which was also elected on a pledge to re-enter the debate on federalism and revisit some of the recommendations of the Sarkaria Commission. But as the 1990s went on, a more stable pattern of bargaining between national and regional interests started to emerge at the central level.

There was a new institutional innovation in intergovernmental relations in this period: the formation of an Inter-State Council (ISC) in 1990 by the National Front Government. The ISC has a permanent secretariat and was set up under Article 263 of the constitution in fulfilment of one of the recommendations of the Sarkaria Commission. The ISC was supposed to serve as a forum to discuss and make recommendations on issues in which some or all states, or the central government and more than one state have an interest. It is constituted by the prime minister, chief ministers of all states and union territories, and six union cabinet ministers. While it played an important role in discussing the recommendations of the Sarkaria Commission, the ISC has failed to serve as an ongoing forum for inter-governmental discussion and coordination. It has met far less frequently than envisaged in the original presidential order, which expected it to meet at least thrice a year. In reality, it has met a total of 11 times since 1990 (in 1990, 1996; twice in 1997; 1999, 2000, 2001, 2003, 2005, 2006, and 2016). After the fall of the National Front government in 1990, it did not meet again until the time of the United Front coalition in 1996. As can be seen from the dates, the Congress party in office has been a less proactive convenor of the ISC than other parties. There are some instances where the ISC has facilitated collective discussion, such as with regards to the rules on inter-state water disputes. But, by and large, it was in the realm of national coalition formation that regional interests came to find their clearest foothold and space for bargaining in Delhi.

From 1998 a steadier pattern of national coalition formation emerged. It was the BJP which first embraced the need to work with regional allies, and through a series of strategic alliances with parties in southern and eastern India was able to form a government for the first time at the helm of a NDA coalition in 1998. While that government collapsed after the withdrawal of a regional ally, a new BJP-led NDA government was elected in 1999 and lasted a full term. It gave way in 2004 to a Congress-led UPA government which survived for two full terms.

How did political regionalisation and the advent of coalition government affect Centre–state relations and the articulation of state interests at the Centre? One major irritant in Centre–state relations declined markedly in use in this period: President's Rule. After the Supreme Court's 1994 Bommai judgment, and as a result of the greater clout of regional parties, the incidence of President's Rule was much lower from the mid-1990s. Many regional parties have participated in coalition governments: between 1989 and 2010, 33 of the 84 parties which won Lok Sabha seats secured representation in cabinet (Ziegfeld 2016, 182). Many of these cabinet posts have been in so-called 'wet' ministries that have offered opportunities for patronage and sometimes illicit kickbacks. Beyond this, there is some evidence to suggest that states governed by regional party allies within national coalition governments secured a greater share of discretionary fiscal transfers from the Centre. Yet, while participation in coalition government benefited certain states and buoyed the fortunes of regional parties, those regional parties which participated in coalition government were rarely consistent proponents for the rights of India's states more generally. This was also not an era of much greater institutionalisation of mechanisms of intergovernmental collaboration or negotiation. Instead—much as had happened during the era of Congress pre-eminence—it was the party system that was the predominant forum for negotiating Centre–state relations.

In the 1990s, economic liberalisation saw the central government retreat from areas where it had previously loomed large. As well as dismantling its position as the apex of industrial planning, the central government also retreated from other commitments as it retrenched spending. For instance, the Public Distribution System (PDS) was scaled back from a universal scheme funded by the central government to a scheme targeted only to below poverty line households. This left state governments to either subsidise an expanded version of the PDS or carry much of the blame for retrenchment. As the central government retreated from some of its role in welfare provision, this opened space for greater policy experimentation at the state level. In the 2000s, as economic growth took off, the central government under the Congress-led UPA attempted to step back into this space but the situation it faced looked very different to earlier phases of Congress rule.

The UPA government (2004–14) used the growing revenues generated by economic growth to initiate a new phase of central spending on anti-poverty programmes, much of which was funnelled to the states via line ministries and centrally sponsored schemes. Centrally sponsored schemes are undeniably a centralised device since they are designed by the central government, yet often deal with issues in the state list. They are also funded primarily by the central government, but can require matched funding from the states. Yet, the hands of central government were tied by the central role played by states in the implementation—and interpretation—of policies on the ground. This was a genuinely decentralised federal polity in which state governments were able to claim the credit for policies even where they were funded or initiated by the central government. The commitment of state governments to implementation of central policies such as MGNREGA was not driven primarily by the partisan alignment of state governments. Many non-UPA-governed states enthusiastically implemented these policies and frequently stole credit for them, much to the frustration of national Congress politicians. The approach of state governments was driven more by prevailing political dynamics within the states.

This was not an era in which the term 'cooperative federalism' was often heard either as descriptor or rallying cry. More often, the central government and the states were in competition with each other. States frequently sought to claim credit in the eyes of voters for development programmes, even where they were centrally designed and financed to a large extent. Many states also sought to push back against the creeping increase in tied or conditional funding from the Centre as they sought to define their own policy priorities.

Post-2014: Re-empowerment of the Centre

Since the return to power of a government in 2014 that is led by a national party with a majority of seats in the Lok Sabha, talk of reinforcing cooperative federalism—and implicitly reinforcing the authority of the central government as a coordinating force—in India has returned. One of the early moves of the new Modi government was to dismantle the Planning Commission. The official mission of the National Institution for Transforming India (NITI) Aayog established in its place in January 2015 is to breathe life into the functioning of cooperative federalism in India. NITI Aayog set out: 'To foster cooperative federalism through structured support initiatives and mechanisms with the States on a continuous basis, recognizing that strong States make a strong nation.' At its first meeting, Prime Minister Modi—the NITI Aayog chairperson—urged states to embrace a spirit of 'cooperative, competitive federalism' in which they would compete with others to improve governance and work in tandem with the Centre to achieve *sabka saath, sabka vikaas* (everyone together, development for everyone).

There has been a profound shift in Centre–state relations under the Modi government. This has been evident both in a renewed usage of the more coercive elements of the Centre's power, as well as a more assertive role in policy design, coordination, and implementation. On the coercive side, the central government attempted to apply President's Rule in two Congress-ruled states in 2016—Arunachal Pradesh and Uttarakhand—where defections or intra-party struggles offered opportunities to challenge the incumbent government's authority in the state legislatures. In both instances, the courts intervened to overturn the attempted imposition.

In the realm of policy, the starkest instance of centralisation was the overnight implementation of demonetisation in November 2016. Many states complained that the means by which demonetisation was carried out—over the heads of the state governments—violated the spirit of cooperative federalism. The political optics of demonetisation were also intensely national and focused on the stature and audacity of the prime minister to make such a bold move. Demonetisation highlighted the extent of the transition in Centre–state relations under Modi and encouraged some opposition ruled states to become more outspoken against the Centre's violation of their terrain.

Another major policy shift of the Modi administration has affected policy implementation: the fulsome embrace and extension of Aadhaar: a biometric identification scheme initiated during the UPA era. Through Aadhaar and the professed goal of moving towards digitisation of the economy, the Modi government has also begun more clearly to challenge the autonomy of the state governments in policy delivery. Aadhaar is being rapidly pushed across states, even those which had not been first adopters and had developed other digital platforms to enable reforms to and better tracking of social provision. This is despite the many concerns about the exclusions that have resulted from the over-zealous attempt to make Aadhaar numbers the basis for eligibility for government programmes including MGNREGA wage payments and subsidised food via the PDS.

Pushing Aadhaar as a unified national platform, as well as experimenting with cash subsidies ('direct benefit transfers') to replace in-kind subsidies, helps to centralise the credit-claiming for government programmes. A similar dynamic is at play with the introduction of the Pradhan Mantri Jan Arogya Yojana (PMJAY)—the prime minister's health insurance scheme—in 2018. These strategies make it harder for state governments to steal the credit for programme implementation and also increase the direct linkage between the individual recipient and the central government, or the prime minister himself.

As John Kincaid observed in the period when calls for cooperative federalism by 'progressive' reformers reached a peak in the USA in the 1950s and 1960s, the term was often used as a rhetorical device to allay fears about centralisation: 'Neither presidents nor Congress could advance reform under a banner of centralization. They had to appeal to cooperation while still cultivating the idea of national electoral mandates as authoritative bases for national policymaking' (Kincaid 1990, 146). In a similar vein, the return to a language of 'cooperative' federalism since 2014 is consistent with a move to re-empower the Centre to set policy agendas and incentivise states to carry out central missions in part through encouraging a spirit of competition among states.

4

Federalism and the Economy

There are some who see competition, as opposed
to coordination, as the most important essence of
federalism. At the heart of this view is the assumption
that governments, like markets, can be organised in
ways that promote administrative efficiency and well-
being through competition. This is a very different
way of approaching the question of federalism
than one that praises the virtue of cooperation. The
Canadian economist, Alfred Breton, one of the first to
articulate a theory of competitive federalism, saw it as
the antithesis of cooperative federalism: 'Co-operative
federalism, if it came to pass, would deny federalism
itself. Those who seek co-operative federalism and
labour for its realization, seek and labour for a unitary
state, disguised in the trappings of federalism, but from
which competition would have been reduced to a
minimum or even eliminated' (Breton 1987, 277).

Influential scholarship in the field of fiscal federalism in recent decades has emphasised the role that federal institutions can play in advancing the dynamism of markets. This model, the basic contours of which date back to the writing of economist Charles Tiebout in the mid-1950s, is premised on the idea that horizontal competition between local governments for mobile capital and labour encourages local governments to act in ways that respond to the problems of business and voters. More recently, since the late 1980s, an influential body of thinking has developed on the 'market-preserving' qualities of federalism. The term 'market preserving federalism' was coined by Barry Weingast (1995) to describe polities which limit the 'degree to which [governments can] encroach upon markets'. Core tenets of the 'market preserving federalism' model include a federal design which gives subnational governments the main role in regulating economic activity within a common market that prevents them from erecting barriers to internal trade. The federal system should also provide incentives for subnational governments to be fiscally responsible rather than rely on the Centre to bail them out.

Enhancing the competitive dynamics of federalism has been one of the key governance reforms sought by India's liberalisers. There has been considerable movement towards a more competitive form of federalism as a result of economic liberalisation.

Central governments, and international actors such as the World Bank, have sought in different ways to enhance inter-state competitive dynamics to encourage states to adopt business-friendly policies that encourage economic growth. This, alongside political regionalisation, has transformed the nature of Indian federalism. It has helped to boost the autonomy of states, as the central government's role as a guiding hand of national economic planning and distributor of public investment has been dismantled.

However, India has not seen a linear process of liberalisation that began at the Centre and radiated through the states once the license-permit raj was dismantled and competitive forces were unleashed. In many ways, there are still strong qualifications on the idea that states have full autonomy to operate, even in areas that are constitutionally designed as state subjects. States remain heavily dependent on the Centre in fiscal terms, even if an increasing amount of public expenditure now takes place at the state level. Fiscal centralisation and the expectation of being able to engage in political bargaining or competition with the Centre continues to complicate the idea that horizontal inter-state competition pushes states to internalise the full costs of their policy decisions. Furthermore, it is at the state level where elite visions of reform agendas collide with mass electoral politics. The central government has to rely on state governments—often with different priorities and capabilities—to regulate the environment in which the private sector operates. Most states remain predominantly rural, and political parties at the state level must balance the oft-competing interests of urban-oriented sectors, farmers, and the rural labouring poor.

States also do not approach the competitive landscape from a level playing field: their abilities to compete are shaped by vast differences in poverty, human capital, infrastructure development, political stability, and the quality of governance. This has been starkly apparent in the era of liberalisation during which regional inequality has increased. Some states have been sites for policy innovation but many more are beset with problems of state administrative capacity that hinder even the implementation of central programmes, let alone creative policy development in response to local needs. On the whole, richer states have grown faster than poorer states, while intergovernmental (Centre–state) fiscal transfers have had only a limited impact on regional inequality.

Governing the Market since Liberalisation: From Centralised to Competitive Federalism?

Economic liberalisation dismantled the role of the central government as the gatekeeper of the license-permit raj. Until the early 1990s, the central government's control of industrial licensing and the freight equalisation policy (which reduced the cost of transporting minerals across the country so as not to disadvantage regions without mineral resources) allowed it to direct flows of public industrial investment with the goal of achieving regionally balanced development. After liberalisation in 1991, states stepped into the breach, taking on a more central role in economic regulation and in competing with each other in the liberalised economy. Liberalisation encouraged inter-state competition for private domestic investment via deregulation, while the reductions of external tariffs gradually enhanced the exposure of states to international competition and potential flows of foreign investment. In such circumstances, state governments have competed to attract private investment by using their role in regulating land acquisition for 'public purpose', the flexibility to alter state taxes or value added tax (VAT) (between 2005 and 2017), the ability to offer concessions on electricity tariffs as well as direct subsidies.

As liberalisation took root, some wrote of the emergence of 'federalism without a centre' (Saez 2002), and of the transformation of the central government's role from an 'interventionist tutelary state' to a 'regulatory state of a federal market economy' focused on monitoring subnational fiscal discipline (Rudolph and

Rudolph 2001). The emergent scenario appeared to be more in line with the mainstream assumptions of fiscal federalism literature that decentralised competition between local (or subnational) governments is good for markets.

The introduction of the GST in 2017 took India another step closer to a model of internal competition within a common market by dismantling inter-state taxes on goods and services. The GST introduced standard rates of tax on goods and services (within six bands) across India, departing from a scenario in which over 1,000 tax rates had been in operation across the country. Heralded as 'one nation, one tax', the GST was passed under Narendra Modi's administration but had been in the making for much longer.

Beyond the endpoint of competition, some observers have also persuasively argued that India's federal model aided the process of liberalisation itself, at least in its initial stages. By allowing the central government to play off interests in different states, and to rein in potential national opponents who were themselves in power at the state level, federalism allowed national reformers to proceed with economic liberalisation by diffusing resistance (Jenkins 1999). Federalism also allowed the central government to shift some of the burden of managing the political costs of economic reform to the states. Where the pressure for fiscal stabilisation led to reductions in central expenditure, state governments with revenue capacity could decide whether to absorb some of the shortfall in expenditure themselves in order to maintain programmes or go along with central retrenchment. For instance, when the central government altered the PDS from a universal to targeted scheme in the mid–1990s, state governments such as Tamil Nadu and Kerala stepped in to maintain a more universal programme, and other states such as Chhattisgarh and Karnataka also adopted more generous food subsidies in subsequent years.

Successive central governments, sometimes working closely with the World Bank, have used inter-state competition in an attempt to encourage states to be fiscally responsible and also to adopt 'business friendly' reforms. They have used a number of levers to do so including control over states' ability to borrow on international markets (a policy lever that was not open to central governments in some of the Latin American federations that faced subnational debt crises in the 2000s); fiscal responsibility legislation; state rankings and competitive bidding processes such as for Smart City status in recent years.

The urgency of tackling subnational fiscal deficits was enhanced by the effects of the Fifth Pay Commission's recommendations in 1996 which increased the wages of public sector employees and had a serious impact on the health of state budgets across India. The Fiscal Responsibility and Budget Management (FRBM) Act passed in 2003 established a target for reducing the central government's fiscal deficit to 3 per cent of gross domestic product (GDP) by 2009. States were given strong incentives to pass their own FRBM legislation, committing them to similar deficit reduction by 2009. States that passed FRBM Acts were then able to access a Debt Consolidation and Relief Facility that consolidated their outstanding loans to central government for a 20-year term with a reduced interest burden and gave them a significant debt write-off. By 2006–7, 20 states had enacted their own fiscal responsibility legislation.

From 1996, the central government also permitted a number of states to negotiate development loans directly with the World Bank. These loans committed the states (Andhra Pradesh in 1996, Uttar Pradesh in 2000, and Karnataka in 2001) to policy reforms intended to enhance growth and poverty reduction. The World Bank wanted to use these 'focus' states to encourage other states to adopt market-friendly reforms, while the central government saw the opportunity to use the World Bank to overcome state-level resistance to reforms and the need to rein in state expenditure on subsidies (Kirk 2005). The loans to the three states met with mixed success.

Andhra Pradesh, the poster child for this approach, and an important regional ally of the BJP-led NDA in Delhi, received a total of $1.6 billion in loans from the World Bank in addition to aid from other bilateral agencies, accounting at the peak in 2001–3 for 31 per cent of the total external assistance received by India (Kirk 2005, 299). Andhra Pradesh under Chandrababu Naidu—under both of his terms as chief minister—has consistently been at the forefront of states in his rhetorical commitment to reforms. However, the state has also continuously failed to tackle difficult subjects such as reforms to electricity tariffs, which would require addressing the heavily subsidised power provided to farmers which prevent the state's electricity sector from recovering its costs. Under Naidu, the state has also carefully used its support for NDA coalition governments at the Centre to negotiate fiscal concessions for the state, most recently in 2018, resigning from the NDA to seek special fiscal concessions for Andhra Pradesh to compensate it for losses as a result of bifurcation from Telangana in 2014.

In the aggregate, state finances across India improved markedly in the 2000s. Access to debt relief and a reduction in interest payments, an overall expansion of government revenues as economic growth soared from 2003, and the introduction of VAT at the state level in 2005–6 helped to reduce the combined gross fiscal deficit of all states to below 3 per cent by 2007 and wipe out their current deficit almost entirely (Aktn, Carrasco, Mundle, and Gupta 2017, 8). These macro-economic conditions enabled states to consolidate their fiscal position without solely focusing on reducing expenditure, even though this had been one of the targets of reformers.

As the pace of growth slowed down in the early 2010s in the tailwind of the 2008 global financial crisis, and following a change of government in New Delhi in 2014, the idea of subnational competition as a driver of reforms and economic dynamism returned to the forefront. In partnership with the World Bank, the central government since 2014 started to rank states according to their implementation of a 'business reforms action plan', which mirrors the World Bank's international 'ease of doing business' rankings. Central guidelines prepared by the Department for Industrial Policy and Promotion have set out a series of detailed reform proposals for states to adopt in areas such as land and property registration, environmental regulation, construction permits, labour laws, inspection reforms, commercial disputes resolution, and obtaining electricity connections. These policy areas cut across the state and concurrent lists of the constitution.

In addition, the central government has encouraged states to introduce amendments to central legislation in areas which fall in the concurrent list. This allows the central government to avoid tackling 'difficult' reforms at the national level such as reforms to labour laws making it easier to hire and fire workers, while encouraging policy experimentation at the subnational level. The BJP-ruled state of Rajasthan has been the most active since 2014, introducing amendments to three major pieces of labour legislation in 2014. These state-level reforms in Rajasthan will mean, for example, that employers have to obtain government permission to retrench 300 workers rather than 100 as per the central legislation. The extent to which these reforms will denote real changes on the ground is debatable since so much economic regulation takes place informally rather than according to formal rules. But it is a sign that the optics have again shifted to focus on subnational competition as a driver of reforms and economic dynamism.

Limits of Subnational Competition

There are limits to the extent that federalism in India does have 'market-preserving' qualities. Not only are states unevenly positioned to attract capital, but the interests of state political elites very often trump—and compete with—the incentives generated by inter-state competition over investment. The idea of market preserving federalism assumes that citizens and businesses do move with their feet. There are plenty of grounds to question this. Businesses develop cosy relationships with ruling political elites who bend regulatory rules to favour their interests in return for support in the expensive trade of contesting elections. Citizens do not necessarily move if they are unhappy with service provision. They may instead remain embedded in clientelistic relations with local brokers. For such reasons, state governments may face political economic incentives to drag their feet on reforms that reduce their ability to distribute public resources on a discretionary basis.

The centrality of local politics in shaping state-level economic policies—and the critical role played by the states in the actual implementation of policy—also presents a challenge to the coordination of economic policy at the national level. The central role played by states in governing the economy has enhanced the fragmentation of interest groups across states. It has been much harder for civil society movements to mobilise at the all-India level, for instance, on issues such as the regulation of land acquisition and rights for those who have lost land, the exploitation of natural resources, or the creation of special economic zones.

Because state governments have become the frontline for wooing capital, they have also become the frontline for struggles over the impact of economic liberalisation on local livelihoods. While this has made it harder for civil society organisations or social movements to challenge the terms of national economic policy, the diffusion of resistance has also meant that the reforms process has been refracted through local stories of political mobilisation and interest group organisation within individual states. This has been especially important when it comes to state-level policies for the agricultural sector including subsidies, access to free or heavily subsidised electricity, and periodic pressures for farm loan waivers which often come into direct conflict with the goals of macro-economic stabilisation because of the pressure they put on state budgets. Popular resistance against land acquisition for private sector projects under the moniker of 'public purpose' has also derailed investments, most famously in the case of the proposed Tata Nano car plant in Singur, West Bengal. The plant was subsequently relocated to Gujarat in 2008 following strident protests supported by the then opposition leader Mamata Banerjee.

Many of the second and third generation economic reforms—such as power sector or labour law reforms—have faced powerful opponents in the states. It is these kinds of challenges that have led to the renewed deployment of the language of 'cooperative'—and 'competitive'—'federalism' under the Modi administration which seeks again to enhance central government authority and influence vis-à-vis the states.

A prominent example is the challenge of improving the health of State Electricity Boards, many of which have been chronically loss-making. Electrical power is a concurrent constitutional issue, and improving the performance of the power sector has been a major focus for successive central governments. Yet, political economy factors at the state level have made reforms to the electricity sector phenomenally difficult to achieve. In many states, farmers—an important political constituency—were given heavy subsidies in the 1980s enabling them to access cheap or free electricity. Subsidies, the straightforward theft of electricity, and the political difficulties inherent in regularly revising tariffs, have made it harder for power distribution companies (discoms) to recover costs.

Central governments have repeatedly urged states to take action to improve the financial situation of the 'discoms'. Some states have tried to reform their power sectors but failed. The Modi government's Ujjwal Discom Assurance Yojna (UDAY) scheme, introduced in 2016, is the latest attempt to turn around their financial situation. States must choose to opt in to the scheme which reduces the interest payments of the discoms by moving 75 per cent of their debts on to state governments' balance sheets while the remainder is restructured by banks into low interest loans. In return, state governments and the discoms are expected to become more efficient in power generation and stem losses in order to reduce costs of power generation as well as undertaking the obligation to regularly revise tariffs.

Reflecting the confused set of adjectives that are sometimes appended to federalism in India, the Union minister for Power, Coal, New and Renewable Energy and Mines, Piyush Goyal, described the UDAY scheme as a 'classic example of Comprehensive, Cooperative, Collaborative, Competitive, Consensual and Compassionate Federalism'. He described how,

> the Governments at the States are envisaged to work in complete cohesion and collaboration with the Centre so as to compassionately focus on ... serving the people of India in meeting their power demands. Further, the scheme encourages State Governments to engage in constructive competition amongst themselves so as to achieve the financial and operational turnaround of their power departments and DISCOMs.[1]

[1] See http://pib.nic.in/newsite/PrintRelease.aspx?relid=160157 (accessed 3 May 2018).

Most states have signed up for the UDAY scheme, although some such as Tamil Nadu held out for longer as they sought to negotiate more support from the central government to prevent the state's fiscal deficit worsening and to avoid passing on more costs to the poorest consumers. The performance of states under UDAY has been variable with transmission and commercial losses increasing in a number of states in the initial years. This underlines the importance of subnational politics and political economy factors in influencing how the reforms process plays out on the ground. The UDAY scheme has also pushed more debts on to state budgets. While the FRBM was loosened for two years after discom debts under UDAY were passed to state governments, in the future states will, in theory, have to service the debts from their existing budgets.

Asking states to take on greater responsibility for infrastructure spending, or directly assuming the debts of their discoms, means that states have to make trade-offs between different areas of expenditure. These decisions have the potential to impact social expenditure, an area in which the states have also taken on an increasingly important role since the 2000s. State governments have become the frontline for the development and trumpeting of welfare programmes intended to help build electoral platforms. While too often dismissed in the financial press and reforms literature as 'populist' schemes in which public resources are effectively given away to voters in pre-election seasons, this characterisation offers an incomplete and often misleading picture. A number of states have improved the functioning of welfare programmes or prioritised building administrative capacity to enable more effective implementation of central government programmes such as the MGNREGS.

Such programmes are electorally popular and have been effective in improving rural incomes, but perhaps, most importantly, help to build an awareness of citizenship rights that in the longer term are crucial for improving local accountability mechanisms. Tamil Nadu has stood out for its policy innovation in the social sector in the 1990s and 2000s, joining Kerala at the forefront of those states in which purposive governmental action has ameliorated poverty and helped to build human capital. Other states such as Andhra Pradesh and Chhattisgarh have made striking improvements to the operation of particular schemes. Other states have been less successful either through choice (such as Gujarat) or due to weaker state capacity and the continued pre-eminence of clientelistic modes of politics (such as Uttar Pradesh).

In recognition of the central role of the states in both planning and financing core public services, the Fourteenth Finance Commission in 2015 recommended a major increase in fiscal devolution to provide states—in theory—with greater flexibility in determining their own expenditure priorities in line with local needs and preferences. The Finance Commission increased the states' share of central taxes from 32 per cent to 42 per cent. These changes, when implemented, were accompanied by a reduction in the budget for centrally sponsored schemes. The overall result, however, was a modest increase in the transfers received by the states. This increase in unconditional transfers raised the possibility that some states may choose to reduce their social expenditure in order to free resources for other priorities. So far, there is little evidence to suggest that states have used their new flexibility in this way (see Aiyar and Kapur 2018), but it is still early to discern the longer term effects.

Regional Inequality

Federalism is never a perfect blueprint for managing the economy. Federations come into existence to serve political ends, and—particularly in India's case—to accommodate regional diversity. They are institutional compromises. While India has moved closer towards pursuing a model of competitive federalism since economic liberalisation and with greater energy again since 2014, actually existing federalism does not correspond neatly to the manifestos of the proponents of 'market preserving federalism'.

One of the major constraints on the extent to which federalism has a positive impact on overall economic performance is the sheer and growing extent of regional inequality across Indian states. Regional inequality has worsened since liberalisation, with richer states tending to grow faster than poorer states. While there is still a debate about the causes of differential regional performance, landlocked states and those in which agriculture or manufacturing accounted for a larger share of state GDP appear to have been at a disadvantage, while those with higher levels of literacy and urbanisation had an advantage (see Ghate and Wright 2013, who compare state performance in 1960–87 to 1987–2004).

The boom years of the 2000s saw faster growth among the poorer states too, but this was not a period of catch-up. Inter-state divergence deepened as a result of continued growth in the richest states. While all states grew in this period, those that were more closely integrated with global markets grew fastest including Karnataka, Andhra Pradesh, Maharashtra, Tamil Nadu, and Gujarat. These more globally integrated states were also the states that saw their rates of growth fall during the global financial crisis of 2008–9 (Subramanian and

Kumar 2012). While poorer states picked up their pace of growth in this period—Bihar was often singled out for attention—the reasons for their growth differed. In Bihar, growing public expenditure including on road construction played an important role in boosting state-level growth. This was not then simply a story of the private sector seeking out new markets. Infrastructure and human capital deficits, in addition to state administrative incapacity, all hinder the extent to which a competitive dynamic encourages the footloose movement of capital across states.

Thus, states do not compete on an equal basis within the competitive model of federalism, nor—given the nature of state-capital relations in most states—is capital truly mobile. Rather it is also embedded within local social and political networks, on which it depends for access to state support, as well as flows of labour and credit (see also Naseemullah 2016). Indian capitalism since liberalisation has had two faces: one a more dynamic, competitive face and another that operates in what Gandhi and Walton (2012) characterise as 'rent-thick' sectors such as real estate, infrastructure, construction, mining, cement, telecoms, or media which are more dependent on relations with the state, which either plays a central role in granting licenses or turning a blind eye to illegality. While most states see a mixture of these two forms of capitalism, in some states—especially those that are less exposed to the global economy—the reliance of business on the state is higher.

The emerging picture of investment and innovation in India's federal market economy is therefore not regionally balanced. Certain states have been able to capture benefits. This is also reflected in the spatial concentration of foreign direct investment (FDI) flows or of special economic zones. Some states have very long run advantages that reflect path dependencies stretching far back.

The regionally uneven pace of growth across states has also helped to perpetuate the vast differences in standards of living across Indian states. In 2014, looking at India's 10 largest states, the average person in the three richest (Kerala, Tamil Nadu, and Maharashtra) was three times richer than the average person in the three poorest (Bihar, Uttar Pradesh, and Madhya Pradesh) (Chakravarty and Dehejia 2016). Human development indicators such as maternal and infant mortality, under-nutrition, and education outcomes vary markedly across states. These patterns show some correspondence with per capita incomes across states, but far from an exact one. Political regimes at the state level also play a crucial role in determining the success of states in tackling poverty and achieving improvements in health and education indicators.

In this context, what role does or can the central government play in seeking to reduce regional inequality? One of the main levers is through fiscal redistribution. Centre–state fiscal transfers operate in two main ways: general purpose transfers as determined by the Finance Commission via a share of central taxation, and specific purpose transfers as governed by central line ministries, which include different government schemes and anti-poverty programmes.

Fiscal transfers as governed by the Finance Commission are designed in a way that seeks a balance between compensating for the differential revenue raising capacity of states without reducing the tax effort in either rich or poor states. Poorer states therefore receive more per capita in intergovernmental transfers than richer states; however, they do not receive sufficient funds to fully offset their revenue shortfall. In order to fully offset the revenue disabilities of the poorest state, the central government would need to transfer five times the amount per capita that it transfers to the richest state (Rao 2017). Even if it did so, poor states may struggle to spend more due to their lower state capacity and staffing shortages. This is true too for the specific purpose transfers that supposedly target poverty reduction such as the MGNREGS or the National Health Mission. Analysis of actual central government grant releases under these schemes reveal a pattern of lower transfers to the poorest states where the need is highest but state capacity to utilise resources lower (Rao 2017). However, on some schemes such as MGNREGS which is a demand-driven scheme, in recent years most states have spent more than they have been receiving in compensation from the Centre, which adds an additional fiscal burden for poorer states (Kapur and Chakravartti 2018).

This discussion has illustrated some of the limits to the central government's ability to redistribute income and economic opportunities across states in the era of liberalisation. The resulting landscape is uneven, and the potential for further regional concentration of economic dynamism is very real, as parts of India continue to deepen their integration with the global economy and other parts continue to see patterns of state–business relations that favour local players and undermine competitive dynamics.

Conclusion
The Future of Indian Federalism

Federalism in India, as elsewhere, has been born of political compromises. As we take stock of Indian federalism, we must not lose sight of the reasons that it came into existence. The gradual revisions to the territorial design of the state, and pushes and pulls in relations between the Centre and states, have been immensely important in the process of democratic consolidation in India. Federalism does not offer a perfect blueprint for administrative efficiency or economic management anywhere, but neither would the alternatives.

As we reach the end of our tour of Indian federalism, it is worth looking ahead to the future. In 2014, the return of a single dominant party at the national level for the first time since Indira Gandhi's premiership in the 1970s again highlighted the significance of politics for determining the fabric of federalism in India. The assertion of a more muscular form of nationalism embodied in the projection of Modi as a strong leader—unrestrained by the checks of coalition government—also has a homogenising impulse that is connected to the promotion of the idea of India as a Hindu nation. The BJP under Modi has sought to fuse the consolidation of national political power with a developmental vision. His government has attempted to build the scope for authoritative policy making by the central government by renationalising political debate and developing new institutional mechanisms to secure coordination between the central government and the states. The future of economic dynamism, or of a reforms agenda, is sometimes held to rest on strengthening measures of coordination between the Centre and the states, or streamlining politics to focus on questions of governance. These centralising administrative tendencies sit alongside a more unitary imaginary of Indian identity and a more majoritarian discourse at the national level.

However, this more unitary imaginary is certainly contested. Some of the loudest contestation has come from regional leaders who have promoted forms of strident sub-nationalism as a counterpoint. In turn, these forms of sub-nationalism have often provoked counter-reactions by minorities within states. Other regional leaders have demanded that their state be granted special fiscal concessions or preferential treatment. The heightening of Centre–state tensions in an era of political centralisation reminds us that the political tide will continue to ebb and flow in ways that will shape the functioning of federalism.

Yet, with the noisy concatenation of Centre–state assertions and counter-assertions, it is possible to lose sight of the big challenges facing India in years to come. Whether we have in mind the pursuit of universal health care, the large-scale generation of productive employment, responding to the agrarian crisis or adaptation to climate change, all of these issues require political leaders with skills and imagination. In order to succeed, they will need to foster collaboration and learning between the Centre and states, and among states, within India's interdependent model of federalism.

Further Reading

This short chapter offers a selective guide to further reading, including many of the texts that have inspired the account of Indian Federalism offered in this book. It is impossible to be comprehensive, but I hope the following offers the reader some fruitful avenues.

For an introductory set of essays about the core principles and legal basis of India's federal model, the *Oxford Handbook of the Indian Constitution* (Oxford: Oxford University Press, 2016), edited by Sujit Choudhry, Madhav Khosla, and Pratap Bhanu Mehta, is a very good place to start, especially papers by M.P. Singh, V. Niranjan, and Nirvikar Singh. Granville Austin's *The Indian Constitution: Cornerstone of a Nation* (Oxford: Oxford University Press, 1966) is a classic introduction and close analysis of the debates that led to the framing of the constitution, including four chapters on federalism. Anirudh Prasad,

Centre-State Relations in India (New Delhi: Deep and Deep Publications, 1985), provides a strong overview of the basic structures of Centre–state relations in the Indian constitution and the impact of judicial decisions on Centre–state relations. Madhav Khosla's *Oxford India Short Introduction to the Indian Constitution* (New Delhi: Oxford University Press, 2012) offers a succinct and authoritative treatment of federalism from a legal constitutional perspective.

On India as a 'holding together' rather than 'coming together' federal system and the significance of its origins for the flexible nature of Indian federalism, see Alfred Stepan, 'Federalism and Democracy: Beyond the US Model', *Journal of Democracy* 10:4 (1999). On the general development of models of cooperative federalism in the mid-twentieth century, see A.H. Birch, *Federalism, Finance and Social Legislation in Canada, Australia and the United States* (Oxford: Clarendon Press, 1955). For reflections on how India learned from these models, see concluding discussion in Birch (pp. 291–6). On the freeze in the distribution of parliamentary seats, see Alistair McMillan, 'Delimitation, Democracy and the End of the Constitutional Freeze?', *Economic & Political Weekly* 35:15 (2000). On changes to Indian federalism since the 1990s, see M.P. Singh and Rekha Saxena, *Federalizing India in the Age of Globalization* (Delhi:

Primus Books, 2013); Balveer Arora, K.K. Kailash, Rekha Saxena, and Kham Khan Suan Hausing, 'Indian Federalism', in *Political Science: Indian Democracy*, Vol. 2, ed. K.C. Suri and Achin Vanaik (New Delhi: Oxford University Press, 2013); Chanchal Kumar Sharma and Wilfried Swenden, eds, *Continuity and Change in Contemporary Indian Federalism*, special issue of *India Review* 16:1 (2017).

To situate Indian federalism in comparative perspective, a reader might consult, Balveer Arora and Douglas Verney, eds, *Multiple Identities in a Single State: Indian Federalism in Comparative Perspective* (Delhi: Konark Publishers, 1995), including essays by Verney and Ronald Watts on the parliamentary tradition and federalism in India, or Rekha Saxena, *Mapping Canadian Federalism for India* (Delhi: Konark Publishers, 2002). The *Routledge Handbook on Regionalism and Federalism* (Abingdon: Routledge, 2013), edited by John Loughlin, John Kincaid, and Wilfried Swenden, offers a more general introduction to core tenets of federalism and their application in different political systems across the world including India.

On the design and reforms to federalism as a means to accommodate and recognise India's ethnic and linguistic diversity, see Alfred Stepan, Juan Linz, and Yogendra Yadav, *Crafting State Nations: India and other Multinational Democracies* (Baltimore: Johns Hopkins

University Press, 2010); Katharine Adeney, *Federalism and Ethnic Conflict Regulation in India and Pakistan* (New York: Palgrave Macmillan, 2007); Harihar Bhattacharya, 'Federalism and Competing Nations in India', in *Multinational Federations*, ed. Michael Burgess and John Pinder (Abingdon: Routledge, 2007). On language as a basis for political community and the territorial organisation of the state, see Paul Brass, *Language, Religion and Politics in North India* (Cambridge: Cambridge University Press, 1974); Robert King, *Nehru and the Language Politics of India* (New Delhi: Oxford University Press, 1997); Asha Sarangi, ed., *Language and Politics in India* (New Delhi: Oxford University Press, 2009). Lisa Mitchell's, *Language, Emotion and Politics in South India: The Making of a Mother Tongue* (Bloomington: Indiana University Press, 2009), Sumathi Rumaswamy's *Passions of the Tongue: Language Devotion in Tamil India, 1891–1970* (Oakland: University of California Press, 1997), and Pritipuspa Mishra's 'Beyond Powerlessness: Institutional Life of the Vernacular in the Making of Modern Orissa (1866–1931)', *The Indian Economic and Social History Review* 48:4 (2011), offer rich insights into language politics in different regions of India. On the post-linguistic reorganisation of state boundaries in the Hindi heartland, see Louise Tillin, *Remapping India: New States and Their Political Origins* (London: Hurst; New York/New Delhi: Oxford University Press,

2013); Bethany Lacina, *Rival Claims: Ethnic Violence and Territorial Autonomy under Indian Federalism* (Ann Arbor: University of Michigan Press, 2017).

For reflections on the contribution of federal design to democratic stability in India, see James Manor, 'Making Federalism Work', *Journal of Democracy* 9:3 (1998), and Kanchan Chandra, 'Ethnic Parties and Democratic Stability', *Perspectives on Politics* 3:2 (2005), who make important arguments about the ways in which federal design has served to quarantine conflicts at state level and politicise multiple facets of ethnic identity. On the power-sharing theory of consociationalism and its application to India, see Arend Lijphart, 'The Puzzle of Indian Democracy: A Consociational Interpretation', *The American Political Science Review* 90:2 (1996), and Steven Wilkinson, 'India, Consociational Theory and Ethnic Violence', *Asian Survey* 40:5 (2000). On India's projection of itself as a pluralist polity in its foreign policy, see Thorsten Wojczewski, *India's Foreign Policy Discourse and Its Conceptions of World Order* (Abingdon: Routledge, 2018).

Another feature of India's federal design that in theory offers the potential to recognise divergent views of what membership in the Indian Union entails is the asymmetric status that has been offered to regions such as J&K, Mizoram, and Nagaland over time. On asymmetry in general, see Louise Tillin, 'United in Diversity? Asymmetry in Indian Federalism', *Publius: The Journal of Federalism* 37:1 (2007), and 'Asymmetric Federalism', in *Oxford Handbook of the Indian Constitution*, ed. Choudhry, Khosla, and Mehta; Rekha Saxena, 'Is India a Case of Asymmetric Federalism?', *Economic & Political Weekly* 37:2 (2012). On the operation of Article 370 in J&K, see also A.G. Noorani, *Article 370: A Constitutional History of Jammu and Kashmir* (New Delhi: Oxford University Press, 2011). On Mizoram, see Smitana Saikia, 'Explaining Divergent Outcomes of the Mizo and Bodo Conflicts in the Ethno-Federal Contexts of India's Northeast', unpublished PhD thesis, King's College London (2017); on Nagaland, Kham Khan Suan Hausing, 'Asymmetric Federalism and the Question of Democratic Justice in Northeast India', *India Review* 13:2 (2014). On the more general question of 'hegemonic' control by the Centre in peripheral regions, see Gurharpal Singh, 'Resizing and Reshaping the State: India from Partition to Present', in *Right-Sizing the State: The Politics of Moving Borders*, ed. Brendan O'Leary, Ian S. Lustick, and Thomas Callaghy (Oxford: Oxford University Press, 2001). See also writings by Sanjib Baruah including, 'AFSPA: Legacy of Colonial Constitutionalism', *Seminar* 615 (2010); 'Nationalising Space: Cosmetic Federalism and the Politics of Development in Northeast India', *Development and Change* 34:5 (2003); *Durable Disorder: Understanding the Politics of Northeast India* (New Delhi: Oxford University Press, 2005).

Moving to the functioning of Centre–state relations, the early reflections of Jawaharlal Nehru as prime minister in his letters to chief ministers are invaluable. See *Letters for a Nation from Jawaharlal Nehru to His Chief Ministers, 1947–1963*, ed. Madhav Khosla (London: Allen Lane, 2014). On the functioning of Centre–state relations in the early decades after Independence, Francine Frankel offers a close reading in *India's Political Economy*, 2nd edition (New Delhi: Oxford University Press, 2005). Further, official insights are offered by the reports of the Sarkaria (1988) and Puncchi (2010) Commissions on Centre–state relations.

For an overview of the patterns of political regionalisation which presaged changes in Centre–state relations from the late 1980s, see Suhas Palshikar, 'Regional and Caste Parties', in *Routledge Handbook of Indian Politics*, ed. Atul Kohli and Prerna Singh (Abingdon: Routledge, 2013); Adam Ziegfeld, *Why Regional Parties? Clientelism, Elites and the Indian Party System* (New York: Cambridge, 2016); and on coalition politics, Sanjay Ruparelia, *Divided We Govern: Coalition Politics in Modern India* (London: Hurst, 2015). On the declining use of President's Rule since the mid-1990s, see Anoop Sadanandan, 'Bridling Central Tyranny: How Regional Parties Restrain the Federal Government', *Asian Survey* 52:2 (2012). Ajay Kumar Singh, 'Dynamic De/Centralisation in India, 1950–2010', *Publius: The Journal of Federalism* 49:1 (2019), offers a comprehensive overview of the stability in India's administrative and legislative centralisation over time, despite political and economic regionalisation.

On changes to the political economy of federalism as a result of economic liberalisation, see Lawrence Saez, *Federalism without a Centre: The Impact of Political and Economic Reform on India's Federal System* (New Delhi: SAGE, 2002); Lloyd I. Rudolph and Susanne Hoeber Rudolph, 'The Iconization of Chandrababu: Sharing Sovereignty in India's Federal Market Economy', *Economic & Political Weekly* 36:18 (2001). On the ways in which federal institutions provided the context for economic reforms, see Rob Jenkins, *Democratic Politics and Economic Reform in India* (Cambridge: Cambridge University Press, 1999), and Nirvikar Singh and T.N. Srinivasan, 'Indian Federalism, Economic Reform and Globalisation', in *Federalism and Economic Reform: International Perspectives*, ed. Jessica Wallack and T.N. Srinivasan (New York: Cambridge University Press, 2006). A critique of the application of the idea of 'market preserving federalism' in India is offered by Jonathan Rodden and Susan Rose-Ackerman,

'Does Federalism Preserve Markets?', *Virginia Law Review* 83:7 (1997). An authoritative overview of the political economy of federalism in India more generally, including its fiscal dimensions, is offered by M. Govinda Rao and Nirvikar Singh, *The Political Economy of Federalism in India* (New Delhi: Oxford University Press, 2005).

A number of studies have looked at widening regional disparities in the period since liberalisation, including Montek S. Ahluwalia, 'Economic Performance of States in the Post-Reforms Period', *Economic & Political Weekly* 35:19 (2000); Arvind Subramanian and Utsav Kumar, 'Growth in India's States in the First Decade of the 21st Century: Four Facts', *Economic & Political Weekly* 47:3 (2012); Chetan Ghate and Stephen Wright, 'Why Were Some Indian States So Slow to Participate in the Turnaround?', *Economic & Political Weekly* XLVIII:13 (2013).

Finally, there is a rich literature on economic governance and welfare across Indian states. On the regulatory role of subnational states, see Aseema Sinha, *The Regional Roots of Developmental Politics in India* (Bloomington: Indiana University Press, 2005); Nikita Sud, 'Governing India's Land', *World Development* 60 (2014); Elizabeth Chatterjee, 'The Politics of Electricity Reform: Evidence from West Bengal, India', *World Development* 104 (2018). See also a wonderful essay by Stuart Corbridge, 'The Contested Geographies of Federalism in Post-Reform India', in *Understanding India's New Political Economy*, ed. Sanjay Ruparelia, Sanjay Reddy, John Harriss, and Stuart Corbridge (Abingdon: Routledge, 2010). On the increasingly important role of states in crafting and implementing policies related to social welfare, see Louise Tillin, Rajeshwari Deshpande, and K.K. Kailash, eds, *Politics of Welfare: Comparisons across Indian States* (New Delhi: Oxford University Press, 2015).

List of References

Aiyar, Yamini, and Avani Kapur. 2019. 'The Centralization vs Decentralization Tug of War and the Emerging Narrative of Fiscal Federalism for Social Policy in India'. *Regional & Federal Studies* 29 (2).

Akın, Çiğdem, Bruno Carrasco, Sudipto Mundle, and Abhijit Sen Gupta. 2017. 'Fiscal Responsibility and Budget Management Act in India: A Review and Recommendations for Reform'. ADB South Asia Working Paper Series, 52. Manila: Asian Development Bank.

Ambedkar, B.R. 1948. 'Constituent Assembly of India Debates (Proceedings)', Vol. VII, 4 November. http://cadindia.clpr.org.in/constitution_assembly_debates/volume/7/1948-11-04 (accessed, 29 January 2019).

Appleby, Paul. 1953. *Public Administration in India: A Report of a Survey*. New Delhi: Government of India Cabinet Secretariat.

Austin, Granville. 1966. *The Indian Constitution: Cornerstone of a Nation*. Oxford: Clarendon Press.

Bhattacharjea, Ajit. 1994. 'Speech by Sheikh Abdullah at the inauguration of the Jammu and Kashmir Constituent Assembly', 5 November 1950. In *Kashmir: The Wounded Valley*. New Delhi: UBS.

Brass, Paul R. 1974. *Language, Religion and Politics in North India*, 1st edition. London, New York: Cambridge University Press.

Breton, Albert. 1987. 'Towards a Theory of Competitive Federalism'. *European Journal of Political Economy*, Villa Colombella Papers on Federalism 3 (1): 263–329.

Chakravarty, Praveen and Vivek Dehejia. 2016. 'India's Curious Case of Economic Divergence'. IDFC Institute Briefing Paper Series. IDFC Institute, Mumbai, Maharashtra. http://www.idfcinstitute.org/site/assets/files/10331/indias_curious_case_of_economic_divergence.pdf (accessed, 15 November 2018).

Chowdhury, Rekha. 2000. 'Autonomy Demand: Kashmir at the Crossroads'. *Economic & Political Weekly* 35 (30): 2599–603.

Constituent Assembly of India Debates (Proceedings), Vol. XI, 18 November 1949.

Dasgupta, Aditya, and Devesh Kapur. 2017. 'The Political Economy of Bureaucratic Effectiveness: Evidence from Local Rural Development Officials in India'. SSRN Scholarly Paper ID 3057602. Rochester, NY: Social Science Research Network.

Elazar, Daniel J. 1987. *Exploring Federalism*. Tuscaloosa: University of Alabama Press.

Frankel, Francine. 2006. *India's Political Economy: The Gradual Revolution*, 2nd edition. New Delhi: Oxford University Press.

Gandhi, Aditi and Michael Walton. 2012. 'Where Do India's Billionaires Get Their Wealth?'. *Economic & Political Weekly* 47 (40).

Ghate, Chetan, and Stephen Wright. 2013. 'Why Were Some Indian States So Slow to Participate in the Turnaround?'. *Economic & Political Weekly* 48 (13).

Government of India. 1988. *Commission on Centre-State Relations*. Delhi: Government of India Press.

Jenkins, Rob. 1999. *Democratic Politics and Economic Reform in India*. Cambridge: Cambridge University Press.

Kapur, Avani, and Parma Chakravartti. 2018. 'Mahatma Gandhi National Rural Employment Guarantee Scheme (MGNREGS), GoI, 2018–19'. Budget Briefs. New Delhi: Accountability Initiative, Centre for Policy Research. http://accountabilityindia.in/budget/briefs/download/1818 (accessed, 15 November 2018).

Kincaid, John. 1990. 'From Cooperative to Coercive Federalism'. *The Annals of the American Academy of Political and Social Science* 509 (1): 139–52.

Kirk, Jason A. 2005. 'Banking on India's States: The Politics of World Bank Reform Programs in Andhra Pradesh and Karnataka'. *India Review* 4 (3–4): 287–325.

Lijphart, Arend. 1996. 'The Puzzle of Indian Democracy: A Consociational Interpretation'. *The American Political Science Review* 90 (2): 258–68.

Manor, James. 1998. 'Making Federalism Work'. *Journal of Democracy* 9 (3).

Mathew, Santhosh, and Mick Moore. 2011. 'State Incapacity by Design: Understanding the Bihar Story'. IDS Working Paper, 366: 1–33.

McGarry, John, and Brendan O'Leary. 2011. 'Territorial Approaches to Ethnic Conflict Settlement'. In *Routledge Handbook of Ethnic Conflict*, edited by Karl Cordell and Stefan Wolff. London: Routledge, 249–65.

Naseemullah, Adnan. 2016. *Development after Statism: Industrial Firms and the Political Economy of South Asia*. Cambridge, United Kingdom: Cambridge University Press.

Nehru, Jawaharlal. 1948. *Letters for a Nation: From Jawaharlal Nehru to his Chief Ministers 1947–1963*, edited by Madhav Khosla. Delhi: Allen Lane.

Prasad, Anirudh. 1985. *Centre-State Relations in India: Constitutional Provisions, Judicial Provisions, Recent Trends*. New Delhi: Deep and Deep.

Rao, Govinda. 2017. 'The Effect of Intergovernmental Transfers on Public Services in India'. NIPFP Working Paper Series, 218. New Delhi: National Institute of Public Finance and Policy.

RBI, *Handbook of Statistics on Indian Economy*, 2017–18. https://www.rbi.org.in/SCRIPTs/AnnualPublications.

aspx?head=Handbook%20of%20Statistics%20on%20 Indian%20Economy (accessed, 29 Jan 2019).

RBI. 2018–19. 'State Finances: A Study of Budgets 2018', Appendix 1 'Revenue Receipts of States and Union Territories with Legislature'. https://www.rbi.org. in/Scripts/AnnualPublications.aspx?head=State%20 Finances%20:%20A%20Study%20of%20Budgets (accessed, 22 February 2019).

Rudolph, Lloyd I. and Susanne Hoeber Rudolph. 2001. 'The Iconization of Chandrababu: Sharing Sovereignty in India's Federal Market Economy'. *Economic & Political Weekly* 36 (18) 1541–51.

Saez, Lawrence. 2002. *Federalism without a Centre: The Impact of Political and Economic Reform on India's Federal System*, 1st edition. New Delhi; Thousand Oaks: SAGE.

Singh, Gurharpal. 2001. 'Resizing and Reshaping the State: India from Partition to the Present'. In *Right-Sizing the State: The Politics of Moving Borders*, edited by Brendan O'Leary, Ian S. Lustick, and Thomas Callaghy. Oxford: Oxford University Press, 138–67.

Singh, Mahendra Pal. 2016. The Federal Scheme'. In *Oxford Handbook of the Indian Constitution*, edited by Sujit Choudhry, Madhav Khosla, and Pratap Bhanu Mehta. Oxford: Oxford University Press.

Singh, Manmohan. 'PM's Independence Day speech 2007'. Retrieved from http://archivepmo.nic.in/ drmanmohansingh/speech-details.php?nodeid=551 (accessed, 13 April 2018).

Stepan, Alfred, Juan J. Linz, and Yogendra Yadav. 2011. *Crafting State-Nations*, 1st edition. Baltimore: Johns Hopkins University Press.

Subramanian, Arvind, and Utsav Kumar. 2012. 'Growth in India's States in the First Decade of the 21st Century: Four Facts'. *Economic & Political Weekly* 47 (3).

Weingast, Barry R. 1995. 'The Economic Role of Political Institutions: Market-Preserving Federalism and Economic Development'. *Journal of Law, Economics, & Organization* 11 (1): 1–31.

Wilkinson, Steven Ian. 2000. 'India, Consociational Theory, and Ethnic Violence'. *Asian Survey* 40 (5): 767–91.

Ziegfeld, Adam. 2016. *Why Regional Parties?: Clientelism, Elites, and the Indian Party System*. New York, NY: Cambridge University Press.

Index

About the Author

Louise Tillin is reader in politics at King's India Institute, King's College London, UK. She has been writing about Indian politics for almost two decades, with a particular focus on federalism, democracy, and the politics of social policies. Her book *Remapping India: New States and Their Political Origins* looked at the reorganisation of states in India's federal system, specifically the creation of Chhattisgarh, Jharkhand, and Uttarakhand. She is an editor of the journal *Regional and Federal Studies*. Before joining King's College London, Louise was the Joyce Lambert Research Fellow in Politics at Newnham College, University of Cambridge, UK. She received her DPhil from the Institute of Development Studies, University of Sussex, UK and an MA from the University of Pennsylvania, USA. Before becoming an academic, Louise worked for BBC News as a South Asia analyst.